Tony Greig Test Match Cricket

A personal view

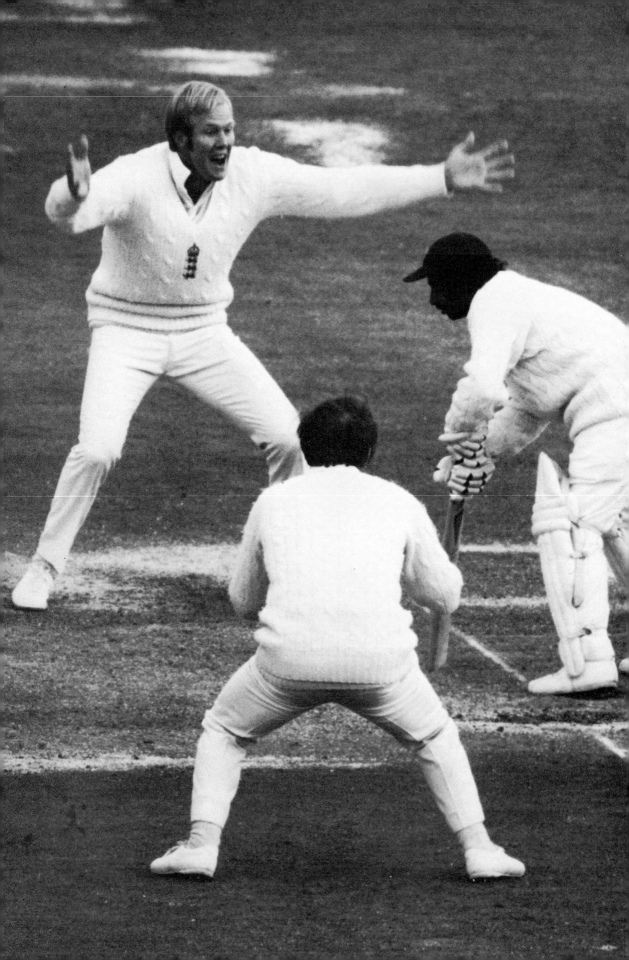

Tony Greig
Test Match Cricket

A personal view

HAMLYN
London · New York · Sydney · Toronto

Half-title page
A jubilant Denis Lindsay after catching Barber for 1 during the England v South Africa second Test at Nottingham in 1965.

Title page
India's Vishy Viswanath bowled by Derek Underwood during the first Test at Old Trafford in 1974. The wicketkeeper is Alan Knott, the fielders John Edrich and myself.

Published by
The Hamlyn Publishing Group Limited
London · New York · Sydney · Toronto
Astronaut House, Feltham, Middlesex, England

Copyright © The Hamlyn Publishing Group Limited 1977

ISBN 0 600 31971 7

Photoset by Tradespools Ltd, Frome, Somerset
Printed by Butler and Tanner, Frome, Somerset

Contents

Setting the Scene

Ken Barrington lbw to Grahame Corling during the England v Australia first Test at Trent Bridge in 1964.

There must have been 80,000 of them. Screaming and cheering, waving and leaping about deliriously. A heaving mass of Indian faces greeting the England side as we trotted around Eden Gardens on an impromptu lap of honour after winning the Calcutta Test of 1977. It was an emotional occasion and I felt drunk with the sweet taste of triumph. Then that thought flashed through my brain – less than six months earlier, I had been on the point of giving it all away.

As England took a fearful beating against the West Indians at Manchester in 1976 and my own batting form staggered from failure to failure, I had almost given up for the first time in my life. Luckily for me, and thanks to the help of Alan Knott, I came to my senses in time to realise the folly of deserting a job that meant so much to me. To captain England is a dream come true; just to play for my country was the realisation of a golden ambition.

Between Manchester and Calcutta lay a chasm choc full of Test match feelings. For, like all the good things of life, Test cricket is a bug that you cannot lose. It can make you a hero and a mug inside 24 hours. It can lift you to the heights of elation, then throw you into a pit of despair. I expect it has always been the same.

The captains of England and Australia, when they first met at Test level in 1876–77, felt the same pressures and tensions, I am sure, as Greg Chappell and I felt as rival leaders for the Centenary Test at Melbourne in March of 1977. But between those two matches there are stories enough to fill a hundred books.

This offering of mine is not intended to be a reference book. I never saw any of the old-time greats and I have drawn on the knowledge and memories of those who did. I have not tried to compile anything like a comprehensive history of the game, more a collection of the events and the men that fascinate me.

Endless comparisons can be drawn between the ages of Grace and Greig and I have attempted to throw some illumination on the differences between playing then and now.

Essentially it is a book of celebration as international cricket raises its bat to salute that first century. It has survived through two world wars, countless riots, no end of controversies. Today it is as appealing as ever.

England and Australia- The Ashes

How can the charred remains of a century-old length of wood bring grown men to tears? Why has a burnt stump created 100 years of controversy, excitement and sensation? The answer lies in two magic words, fading but still legible, on the side of a dark and antiquated urn that will stand forever in the hallowed vaults of Lord's.

As any Englishman or Australian with more than a nodding acquaintance with cricket will certify, there is no feeling like winning The Ashes. To lead England in triumph against the oldest enemy is an ambition that has throbbed incessantly in my brain since early, faltering steps subsequently took me into the first-class game.

Through the annals of the game, strange tales unfold; fuss, panics, heartaches, jubilation, scandals, outcry and sheer heroics. The hidden backcloth is always The Ashes, that glittering prize that can seem as elusive as a myth. But it is there, of course. Just a burnt piece of wood . . .

Part One   Origin and Development: 1876–1938

Emotions can stir with a churning intensity when victory is sighted against the old enemy. Sleepless nights and skipping heart-beats have long been an accepted part of any series between England and Australia—and the pressures do not end with the players.

From the anxious schoolboy fanatic, ear pressed against transistor under the bedclothes for a crackling, dawnbreak hint of progress on the other side of the world, to the distinguished veteran with blazer, striped tie and stick, perched on the edge of his balcony seat, the feeling stays the same. Total involvement.

Spare a thought, however, for one poor chap who drew his last breath amid the drama of one of the earliest Tests. Legend has it, and who am I to argue, that one spectator died from over-excitement during the intense climax to The Oval Test of 1882. Another, lost in the suspense of the moment, is said to have chewed clean through his umbrella.

Opposite
The action of the Australian fast bowler Graham McKenzie.

The Ashes of English cricket which now reside at Lord's.

9

The 1878 Australian cricket team. Left to right (back): J. Blackham; T. Horan; G. H. Bailey; J. Conway (manager); A. Bannerman; C. Bannerman; W. L. Murdoch. Front: F. R. Spofforth; F. E. Allen; D. W. Gregory; W. Midwinter; T. W. Garrett; H. F. Boyle.

True or false, these tales are a colourful sketch of just how forcefully The Ashes can affect the public. I need hardly add that for the players of England and Australia, no other series can produce the same single-minded determination to succeed. I feel sure it was the same in 1877, when Australia won cricket's first Test by 45 runs – and in that far-reaching match at The Oval five years later when The Ashes as such were born.

This was only the second Test match to be played in England, the first, two years earlier, having resulted in a comfortable win for England. This time, however, Australia arrived with their spirits boosted by a 2–0 win over England in a four-match series down under six months earlier. They brought with them a man who was to have a staggering influence not only on this match – and perhaps the unfortunate death of that anonymous spectator – but, indirectly, on the future course of international cricket. His name was Frederick Robert Spofforth, otherwise known as 'The Demon Bowler'.

Spofforth, born in Sydney but of Yorkshire ancestors, was apparently no ordinary cricketer. He stood more than six feet tall, sported a moustache and, from pictures I have seen of him, he wore the same piercing, aggressive stare that we now associate with bowlers such as Lillee and Snow.

Overarm bowling had been permissible only since 1864, which must make Spofforth the first of the world's famous speedmen.

The Demon Bowler. ——(Antipodes.)

Caricature of 'The
Demon Bowler –
(Antipodes)' – F. R.
Spofforth.

Dr W. G. Grace at Gravesend in 1913.

Opposite top
Wilfred Rhodes, the slow left-arm bowler who decimated the Australians in 1902, taking seven for 17.

Opposite bottom
One of England's most successful all-rounders, George Hirst. He played in 24 Tests between 1897 and 1909.

His record of 94 wickets in 18 Test matches justifies his billing, but it is the assortment of stories surrounding the character that, for me, makes Spofforth one of the most fascinating players of early times.

One such story tells that he once rode, presumably on horseback, 400 miles to play in a minor match in Australia. There is no way I could have done that and still felt fit enough to get to the wicket, let alone bowl. But Spofforth? He steamed up and took all 20 wickets, every one of them clean bowled.

In 1878 at Lord's, the Australian tourists destroyed a strong MCC side by nine wickets inside a day. Spofforth's contribution was six wickets for four in 23 balls of the first innings and five for 16 in the second. But it was at The Oval in 1882 that Spofforth achieved immortality in the ranks of fast bowlers.

As Test matches go, this one must rank among the lowest-scoring of all time when you consider Australia totalled 185 runs in two innings – but won! England had been left to make only 85 for victory, and when W. G. Grace guided them to 51 for two, it seemed little more than a formality. Spofforth, who had already bagged seven first-innings wickets and the only two to fall in the second, then apparently came back for a second spell. In 11 overs he took five for 12. England were all out for 77 and Australia had won by seven runs, Spofforth being carried off on the shoulders of his team-mates with match figures of 14 for 90 from 64.3 four-ball overs.

If every game of that age produced such incredible action, it is small wonder that old-stagers view modern-day cricket as slow!

It is now a famous part of cricket history that, on the following morning, the Sporting Times newspaper printed a mock obituary:

In affectionate remembrance of English cricket which died at The Oval, 29th August, 1882, deeply lamented by a large circle of sorrowing friends and acquaintances. R.I.P.
N.B. The body will be cremated and The Ashes taken to Australia.

Within a matter of weeks, the English team were on the boat heading for Australia, seeking revenge. Sure enough, the menace of Spofforth was mastered and after Australia had won the first Test, England took the next two and the rubber. After the third match, a group of Australian ladies ceremonially burnt a stump and sealed the ashes in an urn. That urn was presented to the captain of England, Hon. Ivo Bligh, and transported back to London, where it can still be seen today.

So The Ashes were born. The prize for which the cream of English and Australian cricketers still strain today was the whim of a sub-editor with a sense of humour and a few ladies who evidently saw the funny side.

Amateur Test match bowler Sydney Barnes, comparitively unknown when chosen to go to Australia in 1901.

Spofforth, perhaps the cause of it all, went on playing Test cricket until 1887, then played three seasons with Derbyshire. He lived to be 73 and took to the grave no greater testament to his pace bowling talents than a quote attributed to Edward Lyttleton after facing Spofforth without batting gloves in 1882: 'I give you my word that for several overs I stood on the brink of the tomb'.

If Spofforth was the best-known bowler on the Test scene before the turn of the century, his batting equivalent must surely have been England's W. G. Grace, perhaps the most legendary of all characters in cricket history. Grace is said to have revolutionised batting by playing strokes that no previous player had attempted. It is also said that he was given a standing in England that no cricketer since has matched – and none is ever likely to. In the Victorian age he became a national figure to rival the Prime Minister and the Queen; even now, his memory provokes comical imitations. I once saw Ken Barrington don beard, cap and stomach padding and enter into a mock impression of the famous Grace stance.

Nowadays, then, people may laugh at pictures of W.G. But I am sure there was nothing funny about the man's cricket ability. He scored almost 55,000 runs and took approaching 3,000 wickets in his career, and the fact that his Test match average of 32 is scarcely outstanding can at least in part be pardoned by the generally low scores of the age. On wickets that would nowadays be condemned as unplayable, bowlers dominated; any batsman averaging more than 30 was something special.

W.G. was the fourth of five sons born to a mother who was as keen on cricket as any of them. She nursed their cricketing progress through childhood, supervising their back-door practice sessions like a county coach. Although W.G. became easily the best known, three of the brothers once played in the same England side.

This imposing, bearded man was just 18 when he scored a double-century for an England XI against Surrey and was allowed by his captain to slip off during the match to run in a quarter-mile hurdles race at Crystal Palace. He won, of course. One of his most extraordinary innings must have been the 400 not out he scored in 1876 against a team called 22 of Grimsby. All 22 were fielding! He captained England in their first home Test against Australia and scored 152. Amazingly, he was still opening for England when he was 50 years old and he continued playing in the Gentlemen v Players fixtures until he was almost 60. Who said the England teams of the 1970s are too old?

There are many stories connected with Doctor W.G. somehow combining his medical works with his cricket. No doubt most of them have been exaggerated over the years. But the fact remains that Grace was the first real personality to hit the game. He

Sir Donald Bradman batting at Nottingham during his final Test series in 1948. Godfrey Evans and Bill Edrich are the Englishmen.

managed to command cricket at a time when bowlers were thriving on wicked pitches. The tragedy is that there is no film to show people of our time just how good he was.

In 1899, when Grace played for England for the last time, England and Australia were still visiting each other with great regularity. Although South Africa had by now entered the Test scene, they were by no means up to the standard of The Ashes contestants. So, almost annually, at least one of the two countries faced up to 14 weeks on the sea in a return journey that may have been either a royal adventure or a dip into hell. Somehow, I imagine the players were treated like kings, eating their fill and enjoying wine, women and song. But I may be quite wrong and I am prepared to be told by anyone who was there that these ship journeys were really unpleasant.

It is interesting to think that in the time it took a cricket team to get from England to Australia, an astronaut could now take a spacecraft to the moon and back–and stop off to stretch his legs.

Even as Grace departed from Test cricket, two more greats stepped in. While Grace made a modest farewell with 28 and 1 in the Nottingham Test of 1899, Australia introduced the classical batting of Victor Trumper and England gave a debut to a

15

22-year-old destined to become one of the most prolific all-rounders the world has seen, Wilfred Rhodes.

Trumper died when only 37 and Australia was robbed of a man who might have matched Grace. The marvellous picture of him at Lord's shows the front foot striking out and a huge backlift up above his head. Looking at that picture makes me wonder just how quick the bowlers were at that time, because there is no way any modern batsmen could lift the bat that high against Michael Holding or Jeff Thomson and hope to survive.

Trumper was apparently a batting artist. He was to Australia what Grace had been to England – but whether he could match some of the weird things attributed to W.G., I just don't know. One of my favourite stories of Grace is that he once put the bails back on after being bowled out and prepared to carry on batting. When asked why he had stayed, his reply was simply that the crowd had come to see him bat, nobody else.

Like Grace, Trumper's Test average was nothing stunning – just less than 40. But his finest hour was probably an innings of 104 at Manchester in 1902. Reports of the match relate that the sun was beating down on a rain-soaked wicket – treacherous conditions for any batsman – but that, by lunch, Trumper had scored his century and got out and Australia were 170 for one. That knock provides a contrast with the century I scored against India at Calcutta in 1976 in conditions that were similarly difficult for batting. Trumper took less than two hours – I took eight!

Despite being bowled out for 86 in the second innings, Australia clung on to win that Manchester Test by three runs. Rhodes opened the England bowling with his slow left-arm varieties and took seven wickets in the match. His Test record shows he scored more than 2,000 runs – batting anywhere from one to 11 – and took 127 wickets with an action that, judging by all descriptions, seems to have resembled that of the modern-day left-arm wizard, Bishen Bedi. But the most impressive figure I have seen relating to Rhodes is his striking rate of a wicket every 64.7 balls in Test cricket, in the ranks of the finest spin bowlers bettered only by Jim Laker through the ages of The Ashes. (See striking-rate chart on page 55.)

Perhaps the most compelling duel between Trumper and Rhodes occurred in that 1902 series in England, on the momentous day that Australia were shot out for 36. It was a drying wicket, perfect for the craft of Rhodes, and he ran through the team in less than 90 minutes, finishing with seven for 17. Trumper, however, survived for 70 minutes, scored half of the Australian total and finally fell to Hirst rather than Rhodes.

The previous winter had seen a chain of events which led to an amazing gamble by the England selectors – and the arrival of a man ranked by most records as one of the greatest bowlers, if not

Mike Denness having just lost the England captaincy in 1975.

Stan McCabe (left) and Bradman going out to bat during the England tour in 1934.

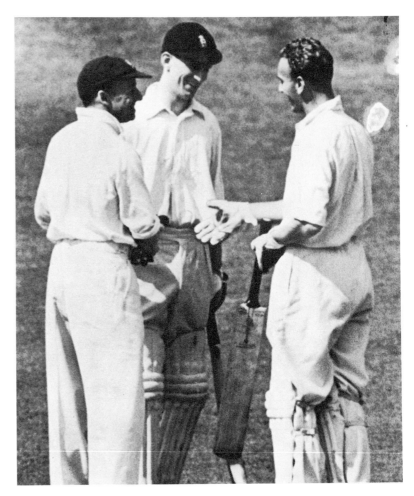

An historic moment as Bradman and Hardstaff congratulate Len Hutton (centre) on passing Bradman's record score of 334 runs at The Oval in 1938.

the greatest, that England has ever produced.

When the team to tour Australia under A. C. MacLaren was being finalised, Yorkshire apparently barred both Hirst and Rhodes from the trip. Stripped of two such accomplished bowlers, England sprang a complete surprise by plucking a player called Sydney Barnes out of the Lancashire League. He responded by taking 19 wickets in the first two Tests before his breakdown in the third cost England the series.

Here is something from the depths of cricket history which deeply interests me, for I believe that the Barnes syndrome is a thing of the future. I want to see the day when doctors, teachers and solicitors can continue with their careers – but if they play well enough, they can combine a professional career with Test cricket, without having to sacrifice everything for the seven-day slog of the county circuit. I honestly believe that the structure of the English game will eventually change to permit such a development, which admittedly seems eccentric today. I cannot, for example, envisage our selectors picking an unknown amateur to face up to Lillee and Thomson in the Jubilee Test of 1977.

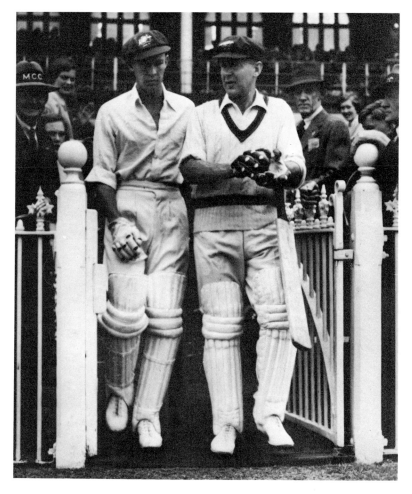

When he was picked for England, Barnes' experience of county cricket was limited to a handful of games for Warwickshire some five years earlier. Subsequently, I understand he played two full seasons with Lancashire, but for much of his Test career he confined himself to the leagues of the north, where he produced some astounding figures. In 27 Test matches he took 189 wickets and our striking-rate comparison on page 55 shows that his Test victims fell at an average of one every 42nd ball; better than Spofforth and better even than the greatest paceman of recent times, Fred Trueman.

Barnes was a curiosity in those times – an amateur Test match bowler – for the trend was very much that bowlers were professionals while many of the batsmen were amateurs. Whether in fact the amateurs played for any financial incentive I cannot say, but the very word amateur can often be misleading – the Australian players even now are termed amateurs and it is no secret that they don't play only for the pleasure. The idea of amateur batsmen continued for many years, however. As recently as the 1950s and early 1960s, Oxford and Cambridge University were

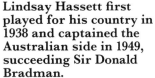
Lindsay Hassett first played for his country in 1938 and captained the Australian side in 1949, succeeding Sir Donald Bradman.

supplying England with batsmen of grace and class, still ranked as amateur. On their beautifully prepared wickets at Fenners and The Parks, batsmen with some natural talent were certain to flourish, and we can thank this system for the likes of Peter May, Colin Cowdrey and Ted Dexter.

Flicking onwards through the pages of Ashes history, the next series to catch my attention was the 1911–12 meeting in Australia. It was preceded by a significant event, the illness of Pelham Warner, forcing the England selectors to substitute John Douglas as captain. In the first Test at Sydney, Douglas chose to take the new ball himself, overlooking the great Barnes, and Australia won by 146 runs. The England team called a conference and Douglas was dissuaded from any repetition. Barnes opened the

Neil Harvey batting for Australia at Manchester in 1953 during the third Test.

attack for the rest of the series, took 30 wickets in four Tests, all won by England, and Douglas came home a hero. He was later to drown tragically when a ship, also carrying his father, was rammed in thick fog.

England's opening batsmen in this series were Rhodes, completing his gradual promotion from the foot of the order, and Jack Hobbs. This great Surrey batsman had made his Test debut in 1908 and he remained England's number one batsman for 23 years. In 61 Tests he scored 5,410 runs, averaging more than 56. But for the seven blank years in Test history caused by the First World War, Hobbs would have set a run record difficult to beat.

Trumper, who died in 1915, was just one casualty of the war years. Many of the great names of the early 1900s were never seen

Ray Lindwall bowling at The Oval during the final Test in 1953. Although Lindwall is remembered as one of the greatest fast bowlers of all time, he also batted well, particularly during the Melbourne Test of 1946–47 when he scored 100 in 115 minutes.

again in top cricket. Even Barnes, who continued playing long after the war, played no further Test cricket. Hobbs continued with a selection of partners, notably Sutcliffe, and from the sea fret and green-tops of my home ground at Hove emerged Maurice Tate, one of England's finest swing bowlers between the wars.

There has been some controversy recently about England teams recalling veteran players. 'Dad's Army' has even been used as a nickname. But we have done nothing to quite rival the move made in 1926 when Wilfred Rhodes was brought back at the age of 48 – and took four wickets to win a classic Test and the series. Rhodes had been playing Test cricket before three of his teammates, including captain Percy Chapman, were born! Both Hobbs and Sutcliffe scored centuries in this match at The Oval, significant for the debut of a wiry, young fast bowler named Harold Larwood, later to become the central figure on the 'bodyline' tour of 1932–33, a series described in detail in another section.

I have no doubts that the bodyline series, and the furore that accompanied it, can be attributed to the little, unimpressive fellow whom I first met in 1971. I have told the story many times

Above right
Keith Miller, possibly the greatest Australian all-rounder in the history of Test cricket. He partnered Lindwall to form a formidable pace combination during the 1948 tour.

of my acute embarrassment at not recognising this figure in a cardigan as the greatest batsman of all time and the man who stood alongside Vera Lynn as my childhood idol – Don Bradman. It will always live in my memory as one of my most unforgivable blunders, and yet Bradman accepted it without a murmur of protest. That this young whippersnapper should assume him to be the organiser of some airport cricket club or another was of no consequence to him. That, for me, sums up the Bradman I know.

He is modest to the extent of being shy, and has avoided controversy like the plague throughout his career. And it never ceases to amaze me, not only that one cricketer can have caused headaches for so many opponents, but that he was also the most unlikely hero you could wish to meet. There is nothing of the lordly presence of a Dexter about Bradman; he is simply a nice guy and surely the man who has come closest to the impossible achievement of perfecting the art of batting.

For one who was destined to rise to such heights, Bradman's Test debut was something of a flop. It came at Brisbane in 1928 against England. Batting at number seven, he scored 18 and one and was promptly dropped for the next Test! He returned for the

Right
Ernie Toshack bowling during the first Test at Brisbane in 1946.

Opposite left
Early cigarette card portraits of Sir Leonard Hutton (above) and Sir Donald Bradman.

Opposite right
Sir Jack Hobbs, England's number one batsman for 23 years after making his Test debut in 1908.

Pages 26–27
I am stumped by Rod Marsh off Ashley Mallett during the Australia v England fourth Test at Sydney in 1975.

third match of the series and, by scoring 79 and 112, took the first steps on the path of a Test career spanning 20 years in which he was never again left out of an Australian side.

Bradman's era featured the great Australian leg-break combination of Clarrie Grimmett and Bill O'Reilly, probably the last leg-spinning pair to appear together for either country. Grimmett was the classical slow leg-spinner, O'Reilly an unorthodox bowler, far faster than his partner. Grimmett took 216 wickets in 37 Tests; O'Reilly, 144 in 27. The men were as different as their bowling: Grimmett small, bony, bald and quiet, O'Reilly a stocky six-footer with views as powerful as his muscles.

The decline of the leg-spinning trade in the wake of this pair has been mourned by many before me and I can only try to offer some sort of explanation. England and India are always unlikely to produce leg-break bowlers of quality and quantity because their home wickets are just not suitable. The accuracy and control of the orthodox left-arm spinner is basically more useful than the leggie on such slow wickets. But Australia, the West Indies and Pakistan should still be able to produce the leg-spinners on their faster tracks – indeed, both Australia and Pakistan have included a specialist leggie in recent years. But even their faith in the craft appears to be diminishing.

Pacemen are progressively taking a bigger portion of Test match overs from the spinners. I think maybe there is an inability to play real pace in Test cricket these days. Certainly, there is assistance for the fast men from the inconsistent bounce in so many pitches.

Modern Test teams are also reluctant to gamble. Just as in football, the trend is to get one ahead and hold it—take no risks unless the opposition equalise. Spinners are basically risk bowlers. They have to gamble, they have to buy wickets—and this applies more acutely to the leg-spinner. So, with one or two notable exceptions, spinners are generally employed in current Test cricket as defensive stock bowlers, killing a few overs while the seamers take a break.

Bodyline was still fresh in the minds in 1936, when England appointed Gubby Allen as captain of the first party to tour Australia since the uproar four years earlier. This, I assume, was partly a political move. Allen had always disapproved of the bodyline theory; he has strong principles and was genuinely against the tactic, so sending him as skipper of the next tour looked like an attempt to patch up the bad feeling and restore relations to a decent footing . . . even if he would have got the job anyway, it proved to be sound judgement by MCC.

Alec Bedser (left) and Doug Wright. England's bowling attack relied on Bedser in 1948, though the 1953 Test series against Australia was probably his finest.

Whatever the aims, the result was a magnificent rubber, watched by the largest crowds ever to attend a series in any country up to that time. The results of the five Tests are worth recording:

First Test (Brisbane)   England won by 322 runs
Second Test (Sydney)   England won by an innings and 22 runs

Third Test (Melbourne)   Australia won by 365 runs
Fourth Test (Adelaide)   Australia won by 148 runs
Fifth Test (Melbourne)   Australia won by an innings and 200 runs

So for the first time in Test history, a side recovered from being two matches down to win a series. Australia, in fact, won the last three Tests by such convincing margins that it seems quite ridiculous they should have been handsomely beaten in the first two; such is the eccentric charm of the game.

Brian Booth run out by
Freddie Trueman
during the fourth day of
the first Test, Trent
Bridge, 1964. As well as
being an outstanding
fast bowler, Trueman
remains one of the
greatest characters in
post-war cricket.

The wickets in that series were open to the weather through
being left uncovered overnight. Some critics of the time have
formed the view that more attractive cricket will automatically
be possible with uncovered wickets, as conditions can change so
dramatically. To me, this is completely wrong. Weather is a
matter of chance and I believe the factor should be eliminated by
complete covering of pitches. Recent changes in regulations have
left us currently with the restriction that only the ends can be
covered – and I have seen some sad and some ludicrous situations
emanate from this law.

Mike Denness lost the England captaincy to me after the 1975
Test match at Edgbaston in which he chose to put Australia into
bat and paid a sickening penalty through being caught on a
'sticky'. As we stood in the pavilion with the rain coming down
and our innings hardly started, Max Walker, the Aussie seam
bowler, said: 'What's going on out there? They haven't covered
the wicket.' Somebody explained that, in England, wickets are

Frank Tyson, the scourge of Australian Test batsmen during the 1954–55 series, still bowling in local cricket in 1971.

not fully covered during Tests, then we all watched while Max convulsed with laughter. No wonder he thought it was such a joke – when play resumed almost two hours later, Lillee and Walker were able to set about us on a wicket that breathed fire and spite. By the end of the day, we were 81 for seven, staggering towards an innings defeat. Mike Denness was soon out of a job, and whatever the merits of his decision to insert Australia, the situation would not have arisen if covering regulations had been in force.

If wickets are covered, and therefore dry, they will encourage the batsmen to play their shots far more readily. Nowadays, they are either worrying about whether it will rain, or about what effect the rain has had. They are inhibited by a regulation that is hindering our chances of producing Test match batsmen.

Dry wickets also encourage spinners, and we all want to see more of them. Damp and slow wickets which currently predominate in England make life easy for the monotony bowlers –

Wally Grout (wicket-keeper) and Neil Harvey appeal for Peter May's wicket during the 1958–59 England tour of Australia, captained by May.

the medium-pace trundlers who can just drop the ball on a length and let the pitch do the rest. This sort of cricket drives crowds away from the grounds at a time when we are trying desperately to keep the game appealing.

In 1937, however, after such a thrilling series, I can excuse those who imagined they had struck on the perfect formula for adventurous cricket. Personally, I am far more inclined to believe that the excitement of the series was produced by the captains, Bradman and Allen, men who played the game in a spirit of flair and aggression.

The final Ashes series before the second war interruption was in 1938 in England. The first Test alone contained five single centuries and two double-hundreds, one of which – from Australia's Stan McCabe – is rated by Bradman as the greatest Test innings he has ever seen.

McCabe's figures lend all the illustration necessary to the innings. He scored 232 in less than four hours, while seven partners

34

Left
**Colin Cowdrey in 1974—
his standards of batting
and behaviour are an
example to all less
experienced players.**

Right
**As well as being one of
the best slow left-arm
bowlers of the post-war
era, Tony Lock was also
a competent batsman
and brilliant fielder.**

fell for 58 runs. McCabe was last out at 411 after scoring 72 of the 77 runs added for the tenth wicket. With statistics like that, who could dare to dispute Bradman's verdict?

An England double-centurion in the next Test was their new captain, Wally Hammond, 35 yet still playing at his peak. Here is another example of a rich talent cut off by the demands of war. The seven lost years could have taken him to 10,000 Test runs, instead of the 7,249 at which he eventually declared—a record only recently beaten by Cowdrey, who played 33 Tests more than Hammond.

The era ended in one of the most famous Test matches in cricket history. England, trailing 1–0, made a mountainous 903 for seven which still stands as an all-time record score. Australia were then twice dismissed cheaply and England won by a ridiculous margin of an innings and 579 runs.

Records abounded throughout this remarkable Test, but one man's performance stands out like a flashing beacon. Len Hutton, now a knight and a Test selector, scored 364, beating

Bradman's 334 and Hammond's 336 not out as the highest individual Test innings. It took him 13 hours and stands today as an example of complete batting application.

I have come to know Hutton as a dry, humorous Yorkshireman, a mickeytaker who good-naturedly remains envious of the perks available to the modern player. If he had been playing in the 1970s, he tells me, he would be a multi-millionaire. It is an assertion beyond dispute. When Hutton was piling century upon century for Yorkshire and England, he received nothing more than a salary and the adoration of the English public. Any cricketer in modern times who approached his standards would be snapped up as a natural for the commercial market; his future would be secure.

The game itself has changed considerably in the past 30 years. But far more rapid, and ultimately more significant, has been the change in the personalities, their image and their opportunities.

Part Two   The Modern Age: 1946–76

John Arlott's gravel-tone voice fell silent. The packed house at The Oval sat stunned and disbelieving. For five seconds it must have seemed that the world had stood still.

Don Bradman, a man immortalised by his batting, was reduced to the human level in an exit more dramatic than any script-writer's plot. It was 1948, the last Test – Bradman's farewell to the international stage. The audience turned up in their thousands to pay homage, and most of them did not just hope to witness a final hundred – they expected it. But cricket would not allow even its greatest servant to pass away unscarred.

I was a babe in arms, two months short of my second birthday and quite oblivious to the magnitude of an occasion in a South London cricket ground, thousands of miles from my Queenstown home. But in recent years I have managed to patch the scene together in my mind. I have talked to the principal characters, read reports, studied pictures, and listened avidly to the radio commentary.

It is Arlott's commentary more than anything else that has brought home to me the emotions of the moment. As Bradman passed the retreating Sidney Barnes and emerged into The Oval sunshine, the crowd were cheering wildly. Every England player stood in a group near the wicket, applauding Australia's favourite man every step of the way to the crease. Australia were 117 for one, Lindwall's pace having already destroyed England for 52. Bradman's career stretched out behind him, spanning 29 Test centuries and a total of 6,996 Test runs. Whether he knew it or not, he needed a meagre four runs to finish his cricket days with an average for his country of 100.

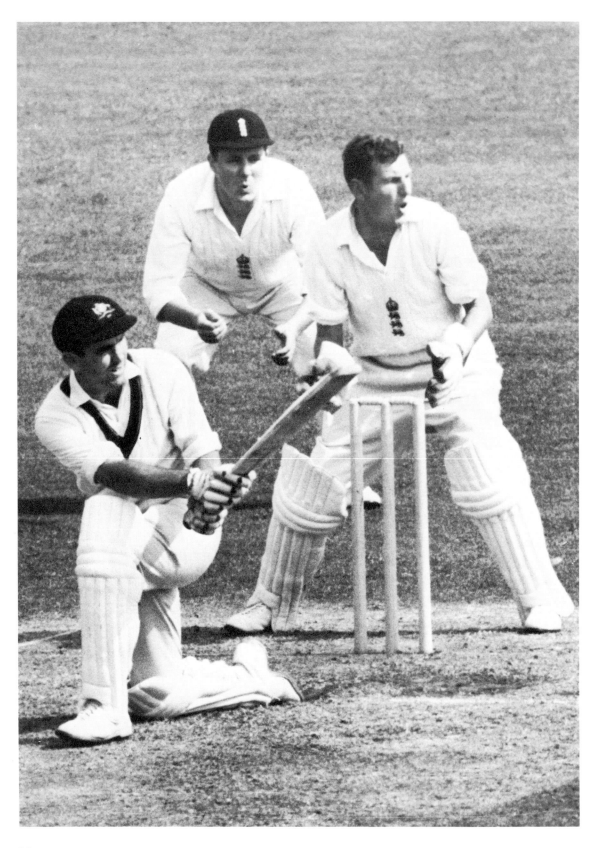

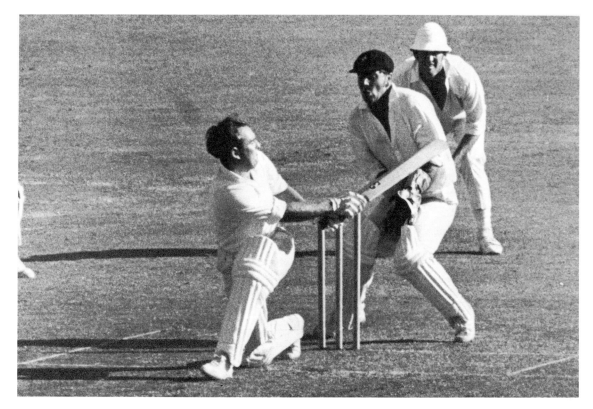

As Bradman prepared to face the first ball there were tears in his eyes, according to the England fielders close to him. Whether that contributed to what followed will never be known. The bowler was Eric Hollies, a cheerful 36-year-old leg-spinner. His first ball defeated Bradman and the crowd let out a thousand sighs of shock and relief combined as Godfrey Evans took the ball. The next bowled him neck and crop.

Arlott, having described the build-up in his inimitable style, observed several seconds' silence as if in mourning at the passing of a genius. Hollies tells me he deliberately bowled a googly and utterly deceived the batsman. Some say Bradman was still in tears as he left the wicket. The crowd, who had stood and cheered only a minute earlier, got to their feet once more and paid their last respects.

There is a startlingly effective photograph hanging in the Melbourne Cricket Ground museum as an eternal reminder of the day that Don Bradman and Test cricket—one of the most success-ful marriages in sporting history—were finally divorced. It shows the little, unimposing figure walking out of bright sunshine, about to enter the shadows cast from the pavilion. From the dazzling brilliance of his Test cricket exploits into the shade of 'retirement'. But there is surely no greater emphasis of the man's reputation than the fact that Eric Hollies will be remembered for years as the man who bowled out Bradman for nought.

Opposite
**Australian captain
Bobby Simpson batting
during the first Test
in 1964 at Trent Bridge.
Simpson is the best slip
fielder I have seen.**

Above
**Captain Ray Illingworth
sweeps a ball to the
boundary during the
1970–71 tour of
Australia. Despite
internal problems
during the series,
Illingworth returned
with The Ashes.**

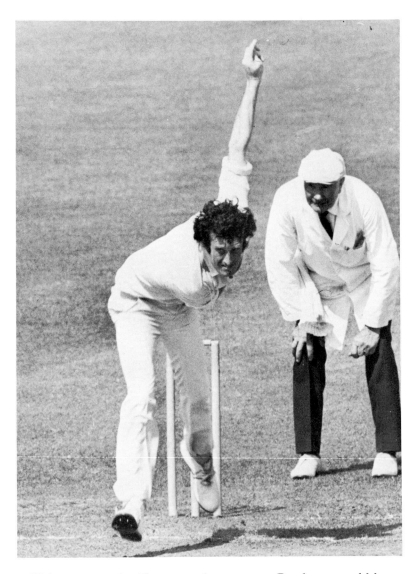

John Snow, the England fast bowler who played a leading role in the successful 1970–71 tour of Australia.

If the moment itself was a sad way to go, Bradman could have asked for no more triumphant series than 1948 with which to say his goodbyes. It has been written that the Australian side that year was the most formidable force to land on English shores since 1066. Their record speaks for itself. Not only did they win the Test series by a thumping 4–0 margin, they also became the first touring team to leave England without a single defeat against country or county.

Apart from Bradman, they had Arthur Morris and Barnes, who both averaged above 80 in the Tests, plus Lindsay Hassett, soon to become captain, and a young Neil Harvey. The bowling spearhead was formed by Ray Lindwall and Keith Miller, the first in a post-war line of pace partnerships to come out of Australia, and support came amply from seamer Bill Johnston (27 wickets in the series) and spinners Johnson and Toshack.

The England side who were defeated so resoundingly looks on paper to be packed with names that the youngsters of today still treat as heroes. Len Hutton, Denis Compton, Alec Bedser, Jim Laker, Bill Edrich and Godfrey Evans were all there, which just goes to show that the greats of every age have to lie down and take their punishment some time. There will be cricketers from every era through history insisting adamantly that theirs was the greatest team. It is easy to believe you are in Utopia as you look back through the mists of time; if we are honest, very few of us have infallible records.

Even when England put their game together, the 1948 Australians were always that bit better. At Leeds in the Fourth Test, England scored 496 to lead on first innings, then declared to set Australia an unprecedented 404 on the final day. They romped home by seven wickets, with Morris and Bradman sharing a second-wicket stand of 301.

Lindwall and Miller, who had first impressed England in 1946–47, shared 40 wickets in the series, Lindwall claiming the lion's share. It is worth comparing these two characters with the most recent of Australian quickie combinations, Dennis Lillee and Jeff Thomson.

Lindwall is the lithe, wiry man with the classical action, like Lillee. Miller is the burly, aggressive bowler with the cavalier image, like Thomson. I have met both men, and found each of them falling into the typically rugged Australian category. Lindwall is now running a Brisbane florists business, while Miller earns his keep with a Sydney pools firm.

While I was in Australia playing for the Waverley club in the winter of 1975–76, I spent a lot of time with Keith Miller, who impressed me enormously with his friendliness. On the field he might have been the belligerent sort but off it he was charm itself. On one occasion, we were together in an outpost of Sydney when he suddenly pointed to a garage and said he remembered some fellow he knew in the war used to work there. The war had been over 30 years, but Miller had not forgotten his old chum. This sort of thing was happening every week! Miller was the big, brash sort that the Australian crowds love. In the war he had seen service as a fighter pilot. From dodging real shells he turned to bowling some pretty powerful weapons of his own.

If one outside factor influenced the series it has to be the ridiculous regulation that allowed a new ball every 55 overs. The law had been changed two years earlier, before which it had been available after 200 runs, and the alteration must rank among the most misguided in cricket history.

Australia were able to nurse their pacemen through their early spells, fill in a few overs with the spinners bowling to defensive fields, then bring back Lindwall and Miller with a new cherry.

Geoff Boycott caught at first slip by Bobby Simpson during the 1964 Test at Trent Bridge.

On average, Australia were taking the new ball with 130 runs on the board. More than once it was taken before England had topped 100. England had nothing to counter with as their bowling attack relied almost exclusively on the great workhorse Alec Bedser. There was not a paceman in sight.

Significantly, the law was changed again the following year to 65 overs. Several further changes were made in subsequent years but I believe we have now arrived at a sensible number with the 85-over rule, which in some countries is modified to 75.

One English cricketer who did not fail in 1948 was Compton, an incredible player who managed to live life to the full. It was a routine that suited his style and he certainly never appeared to suffer. But that, of course, does not mean that every budding young player should try to follow his example. He made his runs in an unorthodox way, just as Alan Knott has done in more recent England sides.

Pages 44–45
Australia captain Ian Chappell lbw to John Snow at Headingley, 1975.

Of Compton's 17 Test centuries, the most courageous was probably his 1948 effort at Manchester. Early in his innings, he went to hook a no-ball from Lindwall and edged the ball up into his face. He was helped off the field for stitching in a gash between his eyes, but with England's innings buckling at 119 for five, he came back to face Lindwall again. Bravery won the day, Compton finished unbeaten on 145 and helped England into their best position of the series before rain washed away their hopes of a victory.

Another lover of the high life in that particular England side was wicketkeeper Godfrey Evans, who today remains one of my favourites among the game's old-timers. Evans simply enjoys life. He is a jolly, mischievous character without an ounce of bitterness in his system and I thoroughly enjoy spending time with him.

The obvious parallel between Evans and Alan Knott, both by coincidence Kentish men, is not one that I care to draw. I never saw Evans keep and can only judge him on his record and his reputation–both very fallible methods. He was undoubtedly, however, the first great wicketkeeper of the post-war days and probably rivalled in cricket history only by Strudwick and Oldfield.

Stories about Evans are ten-a-penny and I once asked him how he managed to retain his bouncy brilliance on the morning after a 'bender'. He replied that it was a simple question of having to. If his customarily agile buoyancy had looked even a little jaded, he said, he could have taken stick from all sides. He wanted to go on enjoying cricket and enjoying life, so he had to make the supreme effort to stay at his sharpest.

England regained The Ashes for the first time in 20 years in 1953 and the achievement was greeted by a moving scene at The Oval. When Compton made the hit that brought England the only clear result of the series, 15,000 ecstatic supporters broke through the police cordon and swarmed in front of the pavilion, calling for captain Hutton.

For Hutton in particular, this must have been a sweet, sweet moment. After suffering heartaches in 1948, and even facing the indignity of being dropped at one stage, he had whipped a side into shape well enough to wrest back The Ashes. But it was a series that could have gone either way throughout its swaying course.

Hassett, Australia's new captain, introduced the umbrella field to Test cricket in this series. I understand that at times he had nine men in an arc from gully to short-leg for the pace assault of Lindwall and Miller. But England had their answer in Alec Bedser, the tireless seamer. Bedser left the previous record wickets tally against Australia for dead with his haul of 39 in the series, and he played a larger part than anybody in the series win. His 14 wickets in the first Test at Trent Bridge staved off a probable defeat while England's batsmen laboured painfully.

The Manchester Test is worth recalling. As usual, it rained, and Australia batted between showers on the first day to make 318. Chief contributor was Neil Harvey, now a matured 25 but still apparently a batsman who would far rather walk the tightrope of failure than defend for six hours. He took frequent risks this time, but scored 122 to justify his means. His attitude to batting is best summed up by one story that tells of a brief but brilliant half-century he made for New South Wales in stifling heat at Melbourne. He came off to a castigation from a selector who said he could have made 300 with more application. 'Who on earth ever wants to make 300?' is said to have been the astonished reply.

Back at Manchester, England replied respectably but by now the weather had ruined the match and only an hour remained when the Australians went in for a second time. In that frantic hour, England took eight wickets for 35 runs!

Leeds staged the fourth Test, which ended in a finale of tension and controversy and exposed one or two loopholes in the game's regulations. On the final afternoon, Australia were left to make 177 to win in less than two hours. Left-handers Morris and Harvey took up the challenge and after 70 minutes they had sent the score racing to 111 for three – 66 needed in the last 45 minutes.

Hutton then closed up the game by setting a three-six field and directing Trevor Bailey to bowl outside the leg stump. The leg theory was successful, Bailey bowling six overs for nine runs, but the Australians, who finished 30 short of their target, were naturally bitter – particularly over Bailey's dawdling which apparently strung out one over for seven minutes. Test match history is dotted with instances of the use of leg theory, all within the rules of the game if not the spirit.

So England escaped and came to The Oval still on terms. First innings totals were close, but Tony Lock and Jim Laker gave early warning of their feats to come by destroying the Australian early order second time round, and England were left to make only 132 to win.

The Australians were introduced in that Oval Test to a man who was to become one of their chief antagonisers in years to come – Frederick Sewards Trueman. He took four wickets in his first bowl against the Aussies, having already scared the life out of the Indian batsmen the previous year.

Judging on records alone, Fred must rate as the greatest fast bowler of all time. His 307 wickets is the highest number by any seam bowler in the world, and he took them at a striking rate of only slightly more than 40 balls per wicket – that is, one in every seventh over. But before making any major statements, it must be added that Trueman took a lot of wickets against teams such as India, New Zealand and South Africa. Alec Bedser, another

candidate for England's greatest seamer, took the vast majority of his wickets against the Australians. On the other side of the coin, Fred often claims that he would have taken 400 Test wickets if he had been picked when he should have been. It is true that he was omitted from two MCC tours when at his peak of form and success and that he was not given a chance to bowl in Australia until 1958, when he was 27.

Trueman is one of the great characters to emerge in cricket, and he remains so today. His views are blunt and forthright, typical of his Yorkshire background, and if there is one memory of his bowling that most people still hold it is of his burning aggression and unstinting strength. I like him as a friend and find his humour hilarious but stories of Trueman have been flogged so consistently over the years that I shan't even attempt to repeat them.

One of the things that still rankles in his mind is being left behind in England when MCC set off for Australia in 1954–55. Frank Tyson and Brian Statham were the fast men selected, and Tyson enjoyed a triumphant tour, his 28 victims including seven for 27 in England's victory at Melbourne—a Test soured by newspaper allegations that the wicket had been watered on the rest day. Fortunately, the ploy, if it took place, helped England's cause rather than Australia's and a major incident was avoided.

Two young university graduates in the England batting order made good impressions on this tour—Peter May and Colin Cowdrey. They were among the last of the England players to progress through the Oxford and Cambridge system that once resembled a conveyor belt into England's middle-order. Both were classical stylists, and although I never saw May bat in person, I have met him frequently since and can class him alongside Cowdrey as a perfect gentleman.

My first experience of Cowdrey was an extraordinary one that I shall never forget. In my first season with Sussex, we played Kent at Hastings—a traditional fixture in those days. It happened that my parents were down from Scotland to watch me, and without a hint or word from me, Colin introduced himself, arranged accommodation and transport and generally ensured that my family had everything that they needed during their stay.

From that day on, I received a number of notes from Colin, usually after I had played a good innings. They would always be full of encouragement—and that, to me, personifies the man. He is a great example to young cricketers, both in batting and behaviour. I know he has had his problems with captaincy and that he has a number of critics. But I can only speak as I find, and Colin Cowdrey rates very high in my personal batting order of cricket people.

Cowdrey still holds the record number of runs in Test cricket

Ian and Greg Chappell, captain and vice-captain of the Australian team which toured England in 1975.

and anyone in future years who challenges his total of 7,865 will be a very special player indeed.

The 3–1 win in Australia in 1954–55 was followed by another England victory in 1956. This is the series that will always be recorded as the property of Jim Laker, who took an unbelievable 46 wickets at nine runs apiece. He won the Manchester Test almost single-handed with an unprecedented 19 wickets, but here I have to qualify his deeds with the evidence of my own eyes.

I have seen a film of the Australians' capitulation at Old Trafford and drawn the conclusion that any ordinary county side could have played Laker better than they did. Their batting was nothing short of disgraceful; they seemed perplexed and quite bewildered by the off-spinner.

Ken Barrington, who watched the match, recalls how Keith Miller would run down the pitch in absurd fashion and pad the ball away with both legs together, quite incapable of countering the Laker menace with orthodox batting. And Ken 'Slasher' Mackay, chewing incessantly as always, apparently signalled complete surrender on one occasion by batting one-handed.

Even these tales cannot detract from the achievement, however, and Laker surely still stands as the finest off-spinner cricket has ever seen, with a striking-rate to justify the honour.

England were now in a run of success, and two winters later they took to Australia what must have seemed a formidable side, with a bowling attack containing five seamers and the world's best spin combination. Trueman went this time, accompanying Tyson, Statham, Loader, Bailey, Lock and Laker in England's bowling armoury. The result? Australia 4 England 0. The reason? According to those who were there, most of the credit for this incredible humiliation of England goes to the man who revitalised the Australian team, their new captain Richie Benaud.

His appointment was a surprise, not least to himself, but Benaud accepted the task keenly, quickly instituting his own ideas and priorities. By all accounts, he inspired the Australians in the field, where they made England look pedestrian, and he led from the front by taking 31 wickets with his leg-breaks.

Benaud is today concerned primarily with television coverage of the game and without hesitation, I name him as the best TV cricket commentator I have ever heard. He is a fair critic and a friendly, helpful man whom I admire enormously.

Ted Dexter was not originally selected for that tour, but when Raman Subba Row was injured, MCC called him up. He interrupted a business commitment in Paris and flew to Brisbane, but on this tour at least, his batting genius was never seen. Many critics thought he should have been included from the start and that his late arrival did nothing to help his chances on his first major tour.

Dexter at the time was 23, just down from Cambridge and apparently a natural for the England middle-order. But my own memories of 'Lord Ted' are much more recent, dating from my arrival at Sussex in 1966.

Meeting Dexter was one of the big things on my mind as I travelled from South Africa to begin my county career. Like so many schoolboys, I had worshipped him from afar, and now I lived in awe of the great man. Frankly, first impressions were disappointing. My father arrived at Hove soon after I had settled in and I thought it a good idea to introduce him. Dexter was sitting in a deckchair reading a newspaper as I walked up, and when I went through the formalities of introduction, he simply lifted his head for a moment, nodded, then went back to his paper. Less than an hour later my faith was restored, when I saw Ted holding my father in earnest conversation near the pavilion.

Out for 96 in my first
innings as England
captain. Second Test at
Lord's, 1975.

Dexter was a man from another age. Somehow he seemed to belong to the era of princes and dashing knights on horseback. But no-one could doubt his talent as one of England's most gifted post-war batsmen. He scored 4,502 runs, averaging almost 50, but may be best remembered for a mere 70 against Hall and Griffith of the West Indies at Lord's in 1963.

Personally, I will remember him best for the style of his come-back in 1968. He had been out of the England team for three years after retiring of his own accord, but suddenly it was rumoured that he fancied another shot. In mid-summer, Sussex were playing Kent and Dexter's name appeared on the team-sheet. He arrived in his own plane, a landing patch having been hurriedly cleared, and strode into the dressing-room followed by a musty smell which turned out to be his cricket bag. Ted, caught by the golf bug, had not touched his cricket kit all season – yet he played that day as if he had been netting daily.

Dexter scored 200 and gave Derek Underwood an almighty hammering. 'Deadly' just did not know what to bowl next as Ted kept driving him back over his head. I have never seen Underwood take that sort of punishment either before or since.

As a captain, Dexter was no great success at Test level, although he did take Sussex to two Gillette Cup victories. In the stages that I knew him, his mind would often wander from a boring patch of the game and he could be seen practising his golf swing in the outfield.

The magic of Ted Dexter lives on today, however. Despite knowing him for years, and rising to England captain myself, I still feel a thrill of importance when in his company.

Dexter's ally in the England middle-order in the early 'sixties was Barrington, as different from Ted as chalk from cheese. Ken was the grafter of the side, never happy to take a risk until he had reached 30, for then, he says, he felt sure he would be in the next Test. He was once dropped from the Test side for scoring a century too slowly, as happened to Geoff Boycott in a later series, but his value to England over the years cannot be overestimated.

Only three Englishmen have scored more than his 6,806 Test runs, only two have bettered his 20 centuries. His highest, and perhaps most valuable innings for his country, was a 256 against the Australians at Manchester in 1964, after Bobby Simpson's 311 had led a march to 656 and left England no option but to save the game. Ironically, Dexter was his partner in a stand of 246.

Barrington is now giving a lot of time and effort back to the game as a Test selector and, in India last winter, he was cheerful, efficient and respected on his debut as a tour manager.

By now, Alan Davidson, Australia's greatest left-handed all-rounder, and Graham McKenzie were operating as Australia's opening attack. I never faced 'Davo' but I have played against

51

Opposite
**Ian Chappell and I
examining the damaged
pitch at Headingley,
1975.**

'Garth' many times. His action is classical, his pace deceptive, and yet he is one of the most gentle, harmless men I have met, without a streak of vindictiveness.

Having won back The Ashes in 1958–59, Australia were to keep them for a span of 12 years, in which their successful captains were Benaud, Simpson – the greatest slip fielder I have seen – and the watchful, left-handed opening bat, Bill Lawry. May, Dexter, Mike Smith and Cowdrey were the England captains who failed; Ray Illingworth was the man who triumphed and brought home the bacon from the 1970–71 tour.

My respect for Illingworth is well known. He is an astute, knowledgeable leader and a players' man. Yet in the preliminary wrangles to the 1970 journey down under, he was appointed late in the day when many expected Cowdrey to take the side. The manager, David Clark, had been named earlier, presumably in anticipation of Cowdrey, and by all accounts there were internal problems during the series – a factor which makes the victory all the more praiseworthy.

England's triumph was moulded around the performances of two men: John Snow, the greatest English fast bowler of my time, and Geoff Boycott, a man who could even now stand alongside all the greatest batsmen in cricket history.

'Snowy' mesmerised the Australian batsmen on that trip. His 31 wickets were 19 more than the number gained by Australia's most successful seamer, 'Froggy' Thompson. It was the highspot in a career that has been chequered, to say the least. Snow has many critics and has brushed with authority frequently. But his talent is such that I have never heard anyone deny his right as the best quick bowler we have produced since Trueman.

To recount exactly my feelings on Boycott would need a book apart. The man who, on this particular tour, averaged almost 100, is currently in a wilderness, away from the pressures of the Test game.

In early November of 1976, I ended a six-week working holiday in Australia and boarded a plane to fly back to England in time for MCC's winter tour to India. The last man I shook hands with at the Melbourne airport was the man who should have been accompanying me all the way to India – Geoffrey Boycott. He had taken up my position as professional with the Waverley club side and was sunning away the winter in Sydney rather than bolstering our batting around the East. To say I felt sad as I said goodbye is an understatement.

Boycott had a straightforward Yorkshire upbringing, and with that fact considered, I can begin to understand the problems which prompted his decision to desert the international scene on which he had thrived since 1964.

Although he obviously always had ability, Boycott was not

born to be a batsman. He was no natural in the mould of a Barry Richards, so he worked at his game. Then worked harder. As a result, he was a boring player in the early stages, obsessed with eliminating risk. Later his style and repertoire of strokes developed and he became a genuinely great player. Then he hit trouble.

Failure was something that Boycott had rarely had to handle. When he encountered it, against the world's quickest men on unpredictable wickets, he found it impossible to tolerate. Although every other player in the England side was struggling just as painfully, Boycott the perfectionist rebelled against the problem and sought peace in leading Yorkshire's county revival.

I have since met him many times, urging him on each occasion to rethink. Whether he will ever change his mind is impossible to say but I now find him a slightly different man, more amiable and less involved in his own batting – at one time he would not be seen for hours if he was out early.

Whatever his motives, it will always be a mystery and a sadness to me that Boycott finds himself unable to go on doing the job for which he seemed destined – to open England's innings for many years. His record of 13 centuries, 65 Tests and an average of almost 50 is already impressive – with maturing skills it could have put him with the immortals.

We have reached the time when I entered the Test arena, at Birmingham in 1972, taking four wickets in my first satisfying day's work against the Australian Test side. The time of Ian and Greg Chappell, of Bob Massie's 16 wickets on his debut at Lord's in 1972, of Dennis Lillee and his partner of later years, Jeff Thomson. The time of Mike Denness, Dennis Amiss, Derek Underwood and Alan Knott.

Of scoring a century at Brisbane against Lillee's full fury. Of watching Lillee and Thomson destroy us four times. Of suffering another defeat at Edgbaston in 1975. Of being made captain and of that magical, unforgettable moment, walking down the steps of Lord's to toss with Ian Chappell. Of scoring 96 in my first day as skipper. Of David Steele, grey hair, spectacles, jutting chin and stubborn grit. Of John Snow's bowling on the second day at Lord's and of the Long Room old-stagers greeting us almost hysterically with the Aussies down and almost out. Of being so close to victory at Headingley and of looking in horror and sick, grinding disbelief at the pitch massacred by the George Davis demonstrators.

These players are still my colleagues or opponents, and the incidents as fresh in the mind as the Centenary Test Match in Melbourne in March 1977. It is awesome to think that we are making history, and are a part of that developing story which began with a burnt stump.

THE ASHES - A POSTSCRIPT

England and Australia's Batting Greats

pre–1914	Tests	Runs	Ave.
W. G. Grace (England)	22	1,098	32.29
V. Trumper (Australia)	48	3,163	39.04

1918–1939			
W. Hammond (England)	85	7,249	58.95
D. G. Bradman (Australia)	52	6,996	99.94

1945–1960			
L. Hutton (England)	79	6,971	56.67
R. N. Harvey (Australia)	79	6,149	48.41

1960–1976			
M. C. Cowdrey (England)	118	7,865	43.45
W. M. Lawry (Australia)	67	5,234	47.15

Bowlers' Striking Rates

The Seamers

Test career		Balls	Wkts	Rate
1876–1886	F. R. Spofforth (Australia)	4,185	94	44.5
1902–1913	S. F. Barnes (England)	7,873	189	41.6
1926–1932	H. Larwood (England)	4,969	78	63.7
1946–1959	R. Lindwall (Australia)	13,666	228	59.9
1946–1955	A. V. Bedser (England)	15,941	236	67.5
1953–1965	F. S. Trueman (England)	15,178	307	49.4
1961–1970	G. D. McKenzie (Australia)	17,681	246	71.9

The Spinners

Test career		Balls	Wkts	Rate
1899–1929	W. Rhodes (England)	8,220	127	64.7
1924–1935	C. Grimmett (Australia)	14,573	216	67.5
1946–1958	J. Laker (England)	12,009	193	62.2
1951–1963	R. Benaud (Australia)	19,093	248	76.9
1966–	D. L. Underwood (England)	15,632	209	74.8
	(accurate to end of 1975)			

West Indies

The West Indian crowd after victory at Lord's in 1973. (On the third day, there had been a bomb scare at the ground.)

Picture the scene. A boat pulls out of a Caribbean port, its cargo including the West Indies cricket pioneers, the first touring team ever to leave the scattering of islands in the Gulf of Mexico for England. Back on the mainland stands a sad, lonely figure, left behind because he could not afford the fare.

That figure was L. S. Constantine, father of Sir Learie. The year was 1900 and Constantine – 'Old Cons' as he apparently became known – had actually withdrawn from the touring party for financial reasons.

The story goes that he was quickly recognised and asked why he had not left with the team. When he gave his reasons, the questioner hurriedly organised a public whip-round in the town and raised enough cash for Constantine's trip. The problem of catching up the team boat was overcome by hiring a speedboat and Constantine was able to join his team-mates on the long cruise to England. There is even a happy ending – Constantine became the first player to score a century for the tourists. And he did it at Lord's against MCC!

That tale draws the sharpest contrast I have come across between the touring conditions in the early days of international cricket and those that prevail now. It also gives an insight into the cricket fever of the West Indian islands, which obviously existed even as far back as 1900.

Antique press cuttings refer to cricket being played in the Caribbean as early as 1806, at the St Ann's Club of Barbados. As is the case with so many countries, it was the British military who firmly established the game, and the Duke of Wellington apparently ordered that a cricket ground should be a compulsory part of every camp.

The negro population were fascinated by the game, but in the early stages the club matches were generally confined to the Europeans. But that first team to England, in 1900, included a number of black, professional bowlers – and eventually a prolific black batsman in Constantine.

Tours were exchanged between England and the West Indies both sides of the First World War until, in 1928, the West Indies

were given Test status. They immediately played a three-match
Test series in England and lost every game by an innings.

On the strength of that disastrous start, it has been written that
it was a mistake to grant them Test status so soon. To me, even
reflecting 50 years later, that was no mistake.

I firmly believe that cricket-playing countries should be introduced to the Test match circuit as quickly as possible. Sure, they
may take a few heavy beatings early on – but how else are they
going to improve? By regularly competing with the world's best
their standards are bound to rise far more rapidly than if they
are left to scramble along in the wilderness. Sri Lanka is a modern-
day example, trying desperately hard to gain acceptance into the
top bracket. I have no doubts that they are not ready, in the sense
that they will not seriously rival Australia, the West Indies and
England at this stage – but I still think they should be given the
opportunity. Despite their early setback, the West Indies seem
to have managed pretty well!

We cannot pass this period of West Indian history without
paying tribute to Constantine junior – the great Sir Learie. On
that 1928 visit to England, he failed with bat and ball during the
Tests, yet managed to score 1,000 runs and take 100 wickets in
the rest of the matches. His most astonishing performance was at
Lord's. He scored 86 and 103 – each in less than an hour – and

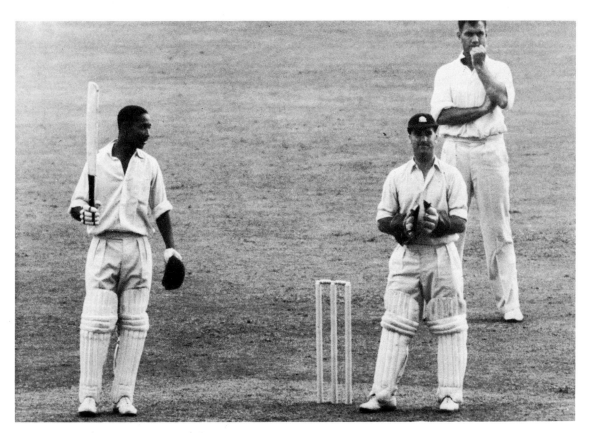

Frank Worrell after scoring 200 runs in the 1950 Test at Nottingham. Evans and Bedser look unhappy about it.

took seven for 57 to secure victory over Middlesex almost single-handed.

I'm told that he was the greatest fielder of all time, but in my book he must have been quite unbelievable if he was better than Colin Bland. Constantine's Test figures do not do justice to his reputation–only 641 runs at less than 20 a time and 58 wickets at 30 runs apiece. But his legend lives on and there seems little doubt that he was the first in the long line of West Indian crowdpullers.

His hitting sounds quite phenomenal, particularly some of his feats at Lord's and the occasion at Canterbury in 1928 when he cleared the famous tree that stood inside the boundary. In later years, he entered the world of politics and won a knighthood. I met him for the first and only time shortly before his death in 1971.

In the same breath as Constantine, I must make mention of the Black Bradman, the man who, until recent exploits by Viv Richards, was the only West Indian batsman with a Test average above 60–George Alphonso Headley.

When I met Headley a few years ago, I found him an un-believable personality, even in his sixties. He told stories with humour and warmth and I found myself transported back to his age–that decade from 1929 to 1939 when Headley never failed in a Test series.

It is said that the West Indies batting line-up was so weak

The unpredictable spinner Sonny Ramadhin.

Opposite
Rod Marsh, Ian Chappell and myself during the second Test at Lord's in 1975.

around that time that if Headley failed, they would struggle to reach 150. That surely makes his phenomenal runscoring all the more remarkable – imagine the pressure of knowing you are the one batsman in the side capable of winning, or even saving, a match.

He made a century on his Test debut, against England in 1929, and mastered the 1930–31 Australian attack to such a degree that Clarrie Grimmett nominates him as the finest on-side player he has ever seen. His last visit to England was in 1939, and he capped it with a century in each innings of the Lord's Test. He finished his career of 22 Tests with 2,190 runs and an average of 60.83.

When cricket resumed after the Second World War, another great West Indian character emerged – a character whose influence was not confined to the field. Frank Worrell, by his strength of personality, achieved the important and complex task of pulling together the islands, making the inhabitants mix and play cricket happily with each other.

The West Indies, of course, are unique on the cricket circuit in that they are made up of several different countries, with separated governments and conflicting policies. As the years have passed, binding them together has become steadily more difficult. Worrell's mighty influence dispersed the problems, but when he retired to the backwoods of the game, troubles arose again.

Now we have the situation in which Guyana and Jamaica are refusing to allow entry to any cricketer who has ever set foot in South Africa. It is a policy that I find illogical, however set on an anti-apartheid route they may be. And my attitude here, as in all situations in which politics tramples on sport, is simply 'what about the public?'

What about all the cricket-lovers of Guyana who long to see Greg Chappell bat? Or the thousands of fanatics from Jamaica who are waiting for the return of Alan Knott? If this policy is continued, those people are going to face a very long wait – with only disappointment at the end of it all. The only crime that Chappell, Knott and a great deal more of the current top flight of Test players have committed, is to play in South Africa. They haven't waved any flags in support of apartheid. They don't want to become involved. All they want, all I want, and all cricket wants, is a freedom of contract that, it seems, politics will not allow.

Worrell, as I have said, did much to help the West Indies negotiate these difficulties during his time at the top. He was also, needless to say, a batsman of the highest calibre and a captain who commanded respect and demanded flair.

He led the West Indies on the two tours that are still remembered today for the rich and exciting cricket that they produced –

Left
**Greg Chappell,
Australian captain in the
centenary year.**

Below
**Barbados – the second
Test against Australia in
1973 at Bridgetown.**

to Australia in 1960 and to England in 1963, his farewell series. In 1964, he was knighted, before graduating to administrative duties in the West Indies.

In addition to being remembered for his individual contribution to the West Indian game, Worrell will be talked about for years to come for his part in the 'Three Ws', the most exciting thing to hit this country's cricket during the 1950s.

The other two members of this formidable triumvirate were Clyde Walcott, the strapping 6ft 2in man mountain, and Everton Weekes, smaller, slighter, but a fierce and spectacular stroke-player.

All three originated from Barbados, the traditional home of West Indian cricket, and were born within a few miles and a few months of each other. Their lives continued this uncanny parallel when all three were selected for their country in 1947. In all, they were to play a total of 143 Tests for the West Indies, each with their definitive styles, yet inevitably linked together by background, brilliance and a letter of the alphabet.

Walcott, who returned to England in 1976 as manager of the West Indian team, began his Test career as a wicketkeeper but later moved into the slips. He was a mighty batsman who loved to hook.

Weekes, so often pictured with his front leg flung aggressively into the air as his bat flails through for another punishing boundary shot, set a record in his first year of Test cricket that still stands today. Just as his poor form seemed to have ruled him out of the winter tour party, Weekes ended his debut series against England in 1947–48 with a century. Subsequently, he opened the tour of India with four successive Test centuries. Nobody, before or since, has struck five hundreds in consecutive Test innings; only two men, Jack Fingleton and Alan Melville, have scored four.

All three of the Ws averaged around 50 with the bat in Test cricket, and Worrell added the advantage of useful fast-medium seam bowling to his many talents. These three men form a major part of their country's cricket past.

They also played a role in launching the famous calypso songs of the West Indies – but not quite such a significant role as did the two most mysterious spinners ever to hit Test cricket, Sonny Ramadhin and Alf Valentine.

Here is a story from the realms of the boys' comics. Ramadhin, a little orphan from Trinidad, and Valentine, a gangling boy from Jamaica, arrived in England in 1950, just after their twentieth birthdays. Valentine had been coached in his home country, but Ramadhin had played only two first-class matches before being picked for the tour. Their success in that tour, and in the decade which followed, is well known. My only regret is that I never saw them weaving their magic.

Ramadhin, judging by the photographs I have seen, must have been an odd sight when bowling, with his sleeves buttoned down at the wrists and his cap jammed on his head. His bowling was odd, too – so odd that no England player on that 1950 tour can claim to have worked him out. Even Walcott, who was keeping wicket, later admitted that he was never sure which way Sonny was going to turn the ball.

The names Ramadhin and Valentine lent themselves admirably to the Caribbean calypsos, and they became the first – and to my knowledge, the only – cricketers to have a hit record written about them.

So the age of calypsos, rum and cricket, lovely cricket had dawned. It still persists today in those islands dotted around the central break of America, where cricket is an expression of life – a joyful life where only the good and happy things matter.

The West Indians are, and always have been, a nation of no half measures, and their cricket sums it up. Their batsman love

67

to smash the ball for four, their bowlers are either very fast or very slow–there is little in between. They either win by a mile or lose by a mile; in cricket, as in life, they are either millionaires or bankrupts.

Somehow, they have managed to retain this flair throughout the years. The trends of stifling entertainment with systematic, mechanical play has not affected them as it has affected other countries–in sports such as soccer and tennis as well as cricket. This is the factor that will always make the West Indies a magical phrase in cricket.

By the mid-1950s, the West Indies had finally been accepted as a considerable force. The preliminaries were past, they were no longer treated with contempt or suspicion, and for the first time, other countries picked their strongest available team when setting off on a tour of the Caribbean.

Then Sobers arrived. He descended on Test cricket in 1954 at

the tender age of 17 years, 245 days. By the time he reached 21, Garfield St Aubrun had made it absolutely clear that he was to be one of the greatest players ever. Whether he is, in fact, the greatest can never be conclusively argued. To my mind, however, he must be the closest to the perfect cricketer in history.

He was still 21 when he scored 365 not out against Pakistan in 1958, still the highest individual score in a Test. By the end of his career, he had become the first, and so far only man to score more than 8,000 Test runs. On top of that, he took 235 wickets in a multitude of bowling styles, and held on to 110 catches in his varying fielding positions.

Even today, Sobers is a god in the West Indies – and rightly so. As I am now captain of England, people may tend to think that men such as Sobers all come the same to me. That is so wrong. Sobers remains a great idol of mine and always will do. I cannot imagine that there will ever be a man to match his talent. He

The historic tied Test against Australia in 1960–61: Wally Grout is run out in the last over with only two balls left and a run still required for victory.

Pages 70–71
Guyanan Rohan Kanhai in the third Test at Lord's in 1973.

batted majestically, bowled seamers as fast as anyone, orthodox left-arm spin and baffling chinamen, and could field with incredible agility in any position.

I believe I also saw his finest innings, and I shall never forget it as long as I live. It was for the Rest of the World against Australia in 1971. It was Sobers' baby, because the World team had been his creation – and now we looked like losing a Test to the Aussies.

Sobers, I recall, said to me with a memorable note of determination: 'I will win this match, even if I have to win it on my own.' I well remember thinking to myself that I believed him, because if anyone in the world could pull it off, it was Sobers.

Well, he went out, scored 130 by the close that day, finished with 254 of the most impeccable runs one can imagine – then came hurtling in with the new ball!

His fielding ability was remarkable, particularly in his short-leg position. His anticipation was uncanny. He could also throw with both arms, by the way, just as an added bonus!

I could talk for hours about Sobers, his skills, and my respect for him as a man. But nothing he ever did comes higher in my estimation than his action on the night of the Kallicharran run-out incident on MCC's 1973–74 tour of the West Indies. The crowd were baying for my blood outside, so Sobers waited with me for four hours, then took me back to the hotel like a guardian angel. I knew I was safe, because Sobers is sacred. Whatever I may have done, nobody would touch me as long as Gary was with me.

We are now into the modern age of West Indian cricket, talking of men who I have met and played against. The age of Wesley Hall breaking into Test cricket with 46 wickets in an eight-match tour in 1958–59, and the age of Lance Gibbs, starting his long and winding road to the top of the Test wickets tree.

Gibbs the bowler, I admire. But I cannot concede that he is necessarily the best spinner of all time, just because he has taken more wickets than anyone else. I'm back to my favourite standpoint – striking-rate – and the fact is that if you bowl enough overs – and you possess reasonable talent – the wickets are bound to come. Lance Gibbs has bowled thousands more deliveries than anyone else in Test history, almost twice as many as Trueman, whose record he passed in 1976.

Ian Thomson, an old Sussex stalwart, who took 100 wickets per season every year for a decade, once advised me that a bowler only has to be good enough to be kept on. If you are kept on, and you bowl 1,000 overs in an English season, you will have 100 wickets in your pocket. Gibbs was always good enough to stay on, good enough to continue with the defensive donkeywork which he did untiringly.

I always enjoy the company of Wes Hall. He is a marvellous

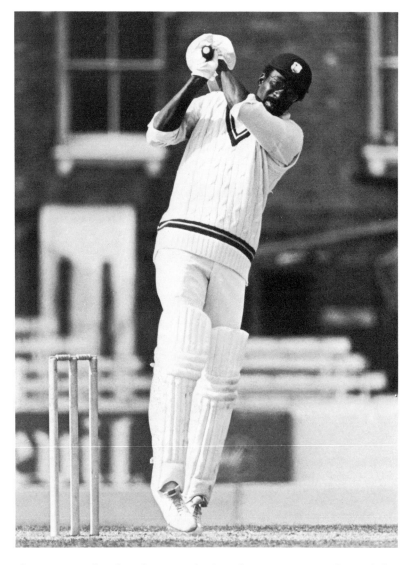

character and, when he was playing, he was a marvellous sight, sprinting in from somewhere near the sightscreen with that lithe, rhythmical action. He took 192 wickets in 48 Tests but my favourite story concerns his religious tendencies.

On one West Indies tour of England, Wes apparently had to bowl at the Reverend David Sheppard. After a few overs, it became obvious that Wes was taking it easy on the Rev, pitching every ball up to the bat. Sheppard was contentedly playing them back. In answer to the inevitable puzzled question from his captain, Wes replied that he couldn't possibly drop the ball short and risk injuring a man of the church.

After much more cajoling, and a few grateful blows from Sheppard, Hall finally cast aside his scruples, let fly a vicious bouncer, and was promptly lashed in the face by the St Christopher that permanently swung around his neck. To this day, Wes

Above left
Captain Clive Lloyd during the 1976 tour of England.

Above
Andy Roberts, Lord's, 1976.

believes that it was an act of God – and he will still show you the scar where the swinging chain struck him.

Hall, Sobers, but not Gibbs, were in the West Indies side that made history at Brisbane on the 1960–61 tour by sharing a tie with Australia. This Test is possibly the most famous ever, but the events are worth recounting yet again.

Sobers began the game with a century out of West Indies' 453; Norman O'Neill then supplied 181 of Australia's 505. With a second innings total of 284, the West Indies left Australia needing a modest 233 to win. That target seemed mountainous, however, when Hall demolished the early batting. At 92 for six, Australia looked destined for defeat, but in the same fearless spirit that had coloured the entire match, Richie Benaud and Alan Davidson belligerently chased victory.

Thirty minutes remained, four wickets still stood and the target was down to just 27 when Davidson was run out. Runs then came at a trickle, and when Hall marched back to begin the final over, six were needed.

The second ball accounted for Benaud. Four balls left, three to win, two wickets up. Wally Grout took a two off the fourth ball, but, attempting a third to clinch victory, was run out by a superb throw from Conrad Hunte. Last man Kline came in and tried to sneak the winning single off the fifth ball, only to become yet another run-out victim as Solomon hit the one stump he could see from square-leg.

The adventure of this match was carried through a memorable series, and the West Indies produced similarly enterprising cricket when they next came to England in 1963. Here again, there is a Test to stir the imagination.

England, left to score 234 for victory in the Second Test at Lord's, reached 116 for three before a lengthy interruption for bad light and rain cut their remaining time to 200 minutes on the final day.

Colin Cowdrey had already been ruled out – or so it seemed – when a short ball from Hall broke his forearm. Now it was the turn of Brian Close, as brave a batsman as any I have seen, to face the fury of Hall and Griffith. Although battered all over his body, Close made 70 priceless runs, and was finally out with 19 minutes left and 15 runs needed. Two wickets remained – but one of these was Cowdrey. When the ninth wicket fell to the fourth ball of the final over, England still being six runs short, Cowdrey walked out with his left arm in plaster. It was an action unrivalled in Test history as far as I know, but fortunately he was not called upon to face, David Allen playing out the two remaining balls to claim a draw.

This 1963 tour was such a resounding success that future schedules were immediately rearranged to accommodate the

Wayne Daniel, Trent Bridge, 1976.

West Indies in England again in 1966, when, under Sobers this time, they again served up some memorable fare.

In the past 10 years, the West Indies have never fallen short of the standard of entertainment they always seem to set themselves. They have not always been successful – in fact, on the 1975 – 76 tour of Australia, billed as the world championship contest, they fell flat on their faces. But this will always be on the cards. It is not within the scope of a West Indian to be predictable; nobody can ever be bored while watching them.

Since Sobers, they have been captained with varying success by Rohan Kanhai, the Guyanan who once delighted crowds by falling over while playing his favoured hook shot, and by Clive Lloyd, one of the greatest cover fielders the world has seen.

Above left
The remarkable Viv Richards batting during the fifth Test at The Oval in 1976.

They have recently been led by the pace bowling of Andy Roberts, now joined by Michael Holding and Wayne Daniel. In 1976 they found a new giant in Viv Richards, who scored more Test runs in a calendar year than any other batsman has ever achieved.

It was Richards, Roberts and Holding who dominated the headlines when the West Indies beat my England team 3−0 in 1976. Yet the Headingley Test of that series will always remain close to my heart. I had been struggling for form and fitness when that Test began, but I came through with a century. It was a match played in the typical character of the West Indies−bold, gay and belligerent. Somehow, defeat loses its sting when the game is played that way.

The spectacular Everton Weekes in action in 1950.

India

Sunny Gavaskar turns
a ball to leg watched by
John Edrich and myself
during the 1974 tour of
England.

The long, dusty drive that connects Delhi's Test Match stadium with the major city road was covered with cricket-crazy Indians. From the radio box on the first floor of the pavilion where I sat with John Lever, it was just like watching a gigantic swarm of ants. But the ants were waiting for us, we had missed the team bus – and there was no other way onto the main street.

This was a December Saturday evening during MCC's 1976–77 tour of India. Lever, playing his first Test at 27, had scored 53 and taken four wickets in a sensational debut day. His name was on everyone's lips and we had just completed a radio interview together for the BBC in London. Now we had the problem of facing the thousands outside and somehow reaching our hotel. I noticed that the prospect had produced a worried frown upon John's normally cheerful cockney face – and I allowed myself an inward smile.

To my team-mate's amazement, I led the way out of the ground and marched through the crowd – then flagged down the first motor scooter that came along. As I had expected, the rider fell over himself to help us. Within seconds, we were on the move – three of us, plus two holdalls, on one scooter.

We travelled about a mile through the cluttered streets, dodging suicidal cyclists, tearaway taxis and blaring horns. The spare wheel at the back was just keeping me on board, but as we threaded our way through more scooters, I had another idea. Tapping our driver on the shoulder, I got him to stop. Then I jumped off and hopped on the pillion of another scooter. Again the rider was pleased to take on boarders and before long we were back at our hotel.

Pages 78–79
India captain Ajit Wadekar about to be caught at third slip by Hendrick during the first Test at Old Trafford in 1974. After losing the series 3–0, Wadekar feared returning to India and never played for his country again.

It had been an unusual journey – and John Lever still found it hard to accept the fact that I had had the 'courage' to face the crowds. But he had not been there before – I had, and I knew the score. That crowd was anything but hostile; to them, we were kings, and we were as safe with them as we would have been on a stroll through a Brighton park.

The sequel to the story surprised even me. The following morning, one of our drivers, an 18-year-old boy, returned to our hotel

with his father, who would not believe that he had taken two England cricketers on his scooter. When I confirmed the boy's story, they gave me a silk tie, a bow tie and a set of handkerchiefs for my wife – presents in appreciation of the honour they felt in being allowed to ferry us home!

That incident did much to help me illustrate the unique atmosphere which Test cricket engenders in India. Nowhere else in the world is a cricketer made to feel so important. Nowhere does a Test match create such fervour.

The adoration syndrome can work in reverse, however – and Ajit Wadekar feared just that after his 1974 tourists had been vanquished 3–0 in England.

No national cricket team enjoys going home after a beating. But Wadekar and some of his men took the apprehension a step farther – for several months after the conclusion of the tour, they refused to go home at all. They lived in fear of the shame and disgrace that would greet them when they stepped back onto Indian soil. Wadekar never played Test cricket again.

It is almost 200 years since cricket became firmly established in India with the formation of the Calcutta club in 1792. Their cricket heritage is naturally British, many of the earliest known matches featuring the Army.

Indian cricket has always retained an aura of royalty. Princes and Maharajahs have dominated their game through the years and I have felt closer than most to this through the characters of Sussex men such as Ranji, Duleep and 'Tiger' Pataudi.

In late nineteenth- and early twentieth-century times, Indian cricket revolved around the great Ranji – full title Colonel His Highness Sir Ranjitsinhji Vibhaji, Maharajah Jam Saheb of Nawanagar – and even now, the country's top state and provincial trophy is named after him.

Neither Ranji nor his nephew, Duleepsinhji, ever played for India, both preferring to turn out for England, where they played county cricket for Sussex. Their legends live on at Hove, where the walls are adorned with their portraits.

Although India did not join the Test circuit until 1932, they had sent their first touring team to England almost half a century earlier, in 1886. This team seems to have been memorable for one feature which very few Indian Test teams have possessed – a bowler of real pace.

The character concerned is one Doctor Pavri. Even the old record books cannot reveal exactly what he bowled, but of his 170 wickets on that tour, two are described in enough detail to convince me of his pace. At Eastbourne, he sent a bail flying almost 50 yards and at Norwich a stump, uprooted by one of the doctor's deliveries, cartwheeled nine yards before lodging in the ground again.

Cricket was introduced to India by the British Army. This picturesque scene is from a match played at Kohat in 1896.

Since joining the Test scene, India have relied almost exclusively on spin, and while they have often boasted the finest spin bowlers in the world, their record has suffered through the absence of fast bowlers.

Now, the wickets are produced to suit spin–not, I am sure, through any devious scheming against visiting teams, but simply because they are not used to anything else.

This is one factor behind the sharp contrast between playing India on home territory, and playing them in India. Their batsmen, with one or two exceptions, are completely perplexed when faced with quick bowlers on a hard and fast track–a combination with which they never have to contend at home.

India will never be a really top-bracket Test nation until she finds fast bowlers–and batsmen who can play fast bowling. It may seem a vicious circle, but the key lies with the wickets. Prepare fast wickets and you will encourage young, quick bowlers. Find quick bowlers in domestic cricket, and your batsmen will be schooled in the arts of playing pace. The result must logically be an all-round improvement in international prospects.

During that first Test tour in 1932, however, India apparently had a very respectably brisk opening pair in Amar Singh and Nissar. And on the June morning at Lord's which marked the start of India's Test career, they both made their presence felt.

Opposite
The West Indies pace bowler Andy Roberts during the England v West Indies fourth Test in 1976.

80

Right
I love touring India, partly due to the rapport I have with the enthusiastic crowds. Here I am batting during the second Test at Calcutta in 1977.

Far right
The finest batsman I have ever played against—South Africa's Barry Richards.

England had named a strong side, captained by Douglas Jardine. But after winning the toss and choosing to bat, they quickly found themselves 19 for three. Nissar had 'castled' Herbert Sutcliffe and Percy Holmes, and Frank Woolley had been run out. Hammond, Jardine and Les Ames led a recovery but England's 259 was scarcely formidable.

Faced with England's pace attack of Bowes and Voce, however, India's dream faltered and they managed only 189. Jardine then declared at 275 for eight and India were bowled out for 187, defeated by 158 runs.

India's first Tests on home ground came in 1933–34, when England played four-day matches at Bombay, Calcutta and Madras, winning the first and third and drawing the second. The discovery of the series was Lala Amarnath, father of Mohinder and Surinder Amarnath, Indian Test players of the 1970s.

Lala made 118 in his first Test and went on to captain India in later years – but only after being sent home from a tour of England in 1936, one of the most sensational disciplinary acts in Test history. Amarnath is still actively involved in Indian cricket as a television commentator.

The Nawab of Pataudi senior led India to England in 1946 and thereby created the unique distinction of having played for both England and India. By that time, his gifts of younger days were fading and he enjoyed little success in the Tests. He died just six years later of a heart attack at the age of 42. If he had lived another 10 years, he would have seen his son follow him to the Indian captaincy.

Along with Merchant, Nayudu and Mushtaq Ali, these were the most impressive characters of India's early Test experience. Then, in 1946, Vinoo Mankad arrived. By all accounts, Mankad is the most accomplished all-round cricketer his country has ever produced, and, as if to underline the fact, he achieved the 'double' of 1,000 runs and 100 wickets on the '46 tour of England.

Mankad then starred in India's first series against Australia – the rampant, mighty Aussies under Bradman. Although Australia won four of the five matches, Mankad scored centuries in each of the two Tests played at Melbourne.

In 1952, he was to perform the sort of individual show that must rank with the greatest ever in Test cricket. It came against England at Lord's and began in style with a six over the sightscreen with the match only half-an-hour old. From that moment, Mankad – who had missed the first Test due to an engagement in a north of England league – dominated the match.

He scored 72 in India's first innings, then delivered no less than 73 overs of slow left-arm bowling for the remarkable figures of five for 196. That sort of output would put most men in bed for a day, but Mankad was on the field again immediately, opening

Duleepsinhji, Ranji's nephew, batting for England against Australia at The Oval in 1930. Bert Oldfield is the wicketkeeper.

the Indian second innings and scoring 184. It was a new record score for the country and it came out of 270 runs scored while Mankad was at the crease. A further 24 overs in England's second innings failed to improve his match reward so he came away with 256 runs and five wickets for 231 from 97 overs. Oh yes, India lost by eight wickets, too!

Unfortunately for India, there was only one Mankad, and the record of the national team continued to be moderate at best and depressing at worst.

Madras, the ground that is still regarded as India's stronghold, staged their first Test match victory, in February of 1952–and Mankad again starred. England, under Donald Carr, looked to be cruising at 224 for five by stumps on the opening day. But after a day of rest–brought forward due to the death of King George VI –Mankad demolished the rest of the innings for 42 runs and finished with eight for 55.

Roy put India's reply on the right road with 111 and a second century came from Polly Umrigar, who was the Indian manager when MCC toured there in 1976–77. England were left with a first-innings deficit of 191 and Mankad took four more wickets as they were whisked out for 183 and beaten by an innings. I can just imagine the scenes of jubilation in Madras that night!

Four months later, however, India were brought firmly back to earth by the debut of Fred Trueman in the first Test of a new series at Leeds.

Lala Amarnath, discovery of the first Test series against England in India, 1933–34. He subsequently became team captain in later years.

Only 41 runs separated the teams in the first innings, but when Trueman set to work again, the game was decided in the space of 14 balls. Three wickets fell to Trueman, another to Alec Bedser, and when captain Hazare went in to prevent a Trueman hat-trick, India were 0 for four – a score never seen before or since in a Test match.

Trueman also decided the third Test at Manchester with a devastating eight for 31. India lost the first three Tests and went home with their tails between their legs. That Madras victory must have seemed an age ago.

By this time, the partition between India and Pakistan was well established, and in 1952 the first of very few Tests between the neighbours was played in Delhi, India sauntering to a win by an innings and 70 runs. Within a week, the tables had been turned, Pakistan winning the second Test in Lucknow, also by an innings. This see-sawing series swung again with a 10-wicket win for India at Bombay which, as the last two matches were drawn, settled the outcome.

Sadly, only two further series have been played between the countries, in 1954–55 and 1960–61, all 10 Tests being drawn. Political conflict has once again come between two sporting rivals and prevented any further cricket – a situation that I find tragic.

India and Pakistan should enjoy the same sort of intense, love–hate competition as England and Australia. One day, I believe, my dream of a world freedom in sport will be realised – and there

Merchant batting during the third Test at The Oval in 1946.

are already signs that the day may not be too far distant when these two countries take the field together again.

When I was last in India in 1976 I heard a story that staggered me – but once again emphasised the complete sporting dedication of the people of this country. An Indian hockey team had travelled to Pakistan for a tour, apparently under instructions to lose, in order that unpleasantness could be avoided.

Indians are so fanatical about sport that they will even go to these lengths to ensure that their relations are kept intact. They just want to play sport and to watch sport. Politics doesn't come into it.

At the end of the 1950s, India entered her most successful age yet. They beat Australia for the first time, at Kanpur in 1959, then achieved their first series victory over England in 1961–62.

India's captain in that triumphant series was Nari Contractor, who was to be fighting for his life in a Barbados hospital just a few months later. Contractor, a left-handed opener, was hit over the right ear by a short ball from Charlie Griffith in the Indian tourists' match against Barbados. A brain surgeon was flown in from Trinidad and Contractor was only removed from the danger list and started on the road to recovery after two major operations. He never played for India again, but did recover sufficiently to play for his zone team two years later.

India lost all five Tests on that tour of the West Indies, and did not achieve their first win in the Caribbean until 1970–71, when Wadekar led them to a surprising 1–0 victory over Gary Sobers' team.

Wadekar, at the time, was a national hero. After the triumph in the West Indies, he brought his squad to England, and repeated the treatment with a 1–0 win over a team led by Ray Illingworth. Suddenly, people began to sit up and take notice of India. Their euphoria continued in 1972–73, when they beat Tony Lewis's MCC team, of which I was a member, 2–1. But in 1974 the party ended dramatically. India were beaten 3–0 in England, hardly offering a challenge, and it was then that I saw the harsh side of their game.

The fanaticism is so great that such a defeat was plainly not acceptable to the public. Wadekar, as I have related earlier, felt unable to face the barrage of criticism that would have greeted his return home. Several of his colleagues felt the same way and stayed in Europe until the passions of shame had at least subsided.

It was the end of a great time for Indian cricket, and the end of a man for whom I still hold a great respect. Wadekar was a fighter–perhaps in the same category as myself–and for that reason I felt a great affinity towards him. He was and still is a likeable man and Indian cricket owes him a great debt.

A. K. Nayudu, another of India's pre-war Test stars.

Wadekar's spot as captain went to 'Tiger' Pataudi, returning to the Test arena under the name Mansur Ali Khan Pataudi. In typically cavalier style, Pataudi inspired India to pull back from 2–0 down to 2–2 in the 1974–75 home series against the West Indies, recording in the process their first victory against this opposition in India. Clive Lloyd's side won the last Test to salvage the series win, but the very presence of this man Pataudi had helped make it tough for them.

Pataudi, another Indian who spent several years with Sussex, falls alongside Dexter in my book as a man whom I feel proud and pleased just to talk to.

For one who virtually lost the sight of his right eye in a road accident in Hove, Pataudi's batting record is brilliant. But I will remember him far more for the regal appearance and personality that set him apart as an Indian cricket prince of modern times.

When Pataudi stepped down, Bishen Bedi, the slow left-arm bowler with bewildering skills, became skipper. His baptism could scarcely have been more fiery, as the new West Indies pace attack of Andy Roberts and Michael Holding ripped into the speed-shy Indian batsmen in the 1975–76 series. 'Bish' was criticised at the time for 'giving up' the Kingston Test after three of his players had been invalided out and two more were nursing injuries. Only six Indians batted in the second innings before Bedi 'declared' to give the West Indies the match. It was a strange incident at the climax of a series that once again highlighted the Indian weakness against pace. But when the MCC team arrived in India in 1976, Bishen had already restored some pride to his team with a win over New Zealand.

Mushtaq Ali batting at The Oval during the 1946 series.

With his brightly-coloured patkas and beguiling bowling, Bedi is one of the great characters of the modern game—and, I can assure you, one of the nicest fellows in cricket.

When he came out to bat against us at Delhi in 1976, I was already clowning to amuse the packed crowd. Having set a man at deep mid-wicket for Bishen's favourite aired drive, I settled down in the slips. But Bish joined in the fun and stepped away from his blockhole to wave the deep fielder a few yards to his left.

The Indian crowd, always receptive to personalities, loved this gesture by their captain and have accepted him as their greatest hero.

Not far behind, however, is the little fellow called 'Sunny'— Sunil Gavaskar. An opening batsman of rich talent and unfailing application, Sunny was mobbed during that Delhi Test when he became the first Indian to score 1,000 Test match runs in a calendar year.

His record for India in recent years is challenged only by a man who stands even smaller than Sunny's 5ft 3in—middle-order man

Vinoo Mankad, India's greatest all-rounder, in action at Manchester in 1952.

Viswanath. 'Vishy', as he is known around the cricketing world, invites a spot of fun by his size, and as I am about 18 inches taller, I have often taken the bait. I always make a point of patting him on the head when he comes into bat, and there is a famous picture of me with Vishy in my arms, curled up like a baby, after he had scored a century against MCC in 1972–73.

The Indian public love to be involved, and they delight in the antics of the top players. I receive some astonishing letters when we are there from fans explaining how honoured they would be to meet me and the other players.

Bedi has received assistance in his slow bowling craft from Chandrasekhar, Venkataraghavan and Prasanna. As usual, spin is the Indian strength in the seventies. But apart from Gavaskar and Viswanath, their batting has often been fragile.

For the sake of the people, who love cricket like no others I have ever seen, I will always wish India well. It has been said that I have a remarkable fascination for the place and I will not deny it. I enjoy being made to feel like a king.

South Africa

South Africa's greatest ever cricket team lived the life of ghosts throughout the early 1970s. We knew they were still around, but nobody was allowed to see them. Now that team is dead, their collectively awesome talent lost to the world.

It will always remain one of the disasters of Test cricket that this side, having slaughtered Bill Lawry's Australians 4–0 as the seventies dawned, was then buried alive by an issue entirely out of the players' control.

Sport was used simply as a political vehicle in the apartheid conflict. Yet most of the players who suffered had already advertised their feelings by staging a planned walk-off during an exhibition match, their own demonstration against the policy that was soon to strip their lives of incentive.

Stalemate now exists in the saddened country where I was born and raised. The public and the players live on in hope, some of them still believing that the day will soon dawn when South Africa can rejoin the international sporting circuit. Others are plainly resigned to the tragedy of it all.

Without wishing to become involved in the ethics and morals of the situation, I passionately believe that a return to sporting relations with the other top countries of the world would give an incalculable boost to the South African public and their desire to do the right thing. So many of the inhabitants still live for sport. If it were possible, they would direct their lives around the cricket, rugby and golf exploits of the nation's stars. Think what a lift international sport would bring to these people, and perhaps what a help that might be to the overall position.

My sympathies go out to the men who have lost most by the events of recent years. To Barry Richards, who could by now have been accepted as one of the greatest batsmen the world has seen, to Mike Procter, robbed of the opportunity to rival the all-round achievements of Sobers. And to the more seasoned players such as Eddie Barlow and Graeme Pollock, who were at the peak of their careers when the door was slammed in their faces.

Even if South Africa took the field against England or Australia tomorrow, they could not hope to make the same impact as

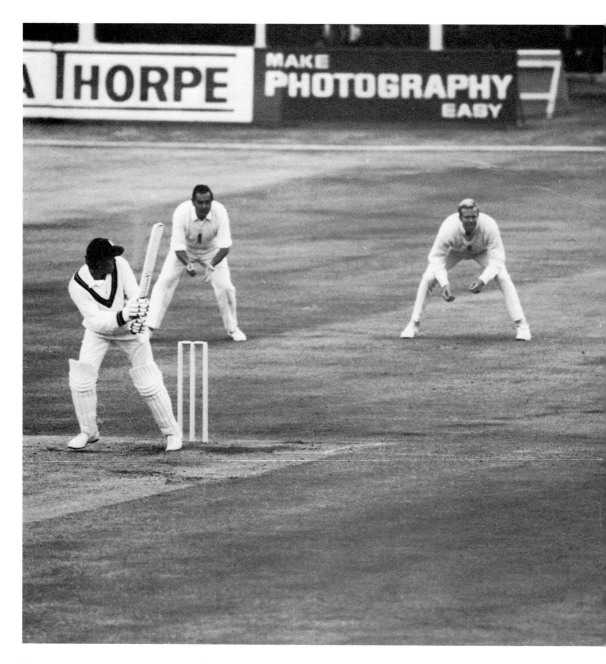

Barry Richards gets a ball past Basil d'Oliveira during the England v Rest of the World second Test in 1970.

the team of 1970. Too many of that side are now retired, or past their best, and replacements cannot be produced at will from a country that has had no international opposition for six years.

The 1970 team, it seems, was a far cry from the first South African side to enter the Test arena, 81 years earlier. For although faced by a touring MCC team of only moderate county standard, South Africa lost their first two Test ventures by convincing margins. It was not until 1905–06 that South Africa seriously challenged England's superiority – and then they did it so well that they won four Tests in a five-match series!

Names such as Mitchell, Sinclair, the all-rounder Faulkner and the pioneer googly bowlers Schwarz and Vogler dominated South African cricket in the early part of the twentieth century.

Then Herby Taylor emerged and quickly became the country's most accomplished batsman. There are still those today who rank him as technically the country's finest player of all time. Taylor enjoyed some fierce duels with England's wonder bowler Sydney Barnes during MCC's 1913–14 tour. Barnes wrecked South Africa by taking 49 wickets in four Tests, yet Taylor emerged with scores of 109, 93 and 87. The war interrupted his masterful career but he still bowed out with 42 Test caps and an average of more than 40.

Taylor's greatest innings were played on the matting wickets of South Africa. It is said that when turf took over his talent seemed diminished–certainly, it must have been a period of adaptation for all South African cricketers when grass became the accepted surface early in the 1930s.

South Africa scored her first series win in England in 1935 but met swift disillusionment against the 1935–36 Australians, who won 10 of 16 matches by an innings. Only one memory stands out in the minds of those who saw that tour from South Africa's side of the fence–and that is a wonderful double-century by Dudley Nourse in the second Test at Johannesburg.

This was to be the highest score in a career of 34 Tests and almost 3,000 runs by Nourse, the son of an equally famous South African player. But the innings of his life must have been at Trent Bridge in 1951, when he was captaining South Africa against England. His thumb was broken even before he walked out to bat, yet, with every stroke bringing agony, he stayed more than nine hours to score 208 and lay the foundations for a shock South African victory.

That, however, was 12 years after the most extraordinary match in South Africa's history–the timeless Test at Durban in 1939. It was a guinea-pig match, continuing the experiment of setting no time limit. As such, it must rank as a failure because no definite result was achieved. But it is a story well worth telling and a match that I still love to read about now.

South Africa, winning the toss for the first time in the series, batted well into the third day for 530 and might have been excused for thinking themselves reasonably safe. Their optimism of salvaging the series with a victory must have grown when they bowled England out for 316 by lunch on the fifth day. Instead of enforcing the follow-on, Alan Melville, who is now a cricket broadcaster, opted to bat again, and scored a century himself out of 481. England were set to score 696 runs to win.

Paul Gibb and Bill Edrich batted for most of the seventh day and when bad light intervened, England were 253 for one. Rain

Herby Taylor, considered by some to be the finest player South Africa has ever produced.

washed out the eighth day, but Gibb then completed a century – then the slowest in the history of Tests – and was finally out for 120 after 7½ hours. Edrich marched on to 219, captain Hammond scored 140 and by tea on the tenth day, England were an unbelievable 654 for five, a record fourth-innings score and only 42 short of victory.

Although no finishing date had been scheduled, the game was then cut off at its climax – because the England team had to catch the boat home! That really is the weirdest reason I have ever heard for a cricket match to finish and I still wonder why the boat could not have been delayed while 42 runs were scored. Apparently, this was the second occasion on which an England team had sailed away from a timeless Test – it first happened in Jamaica 10 years earlier when the West Indies, set no less than 849, were 408 for five after nine days.

After the war, South Africa launched into a fabulously successful spell, with Nourse still playing beautifully and Hughie Tayfield casting spells with his off-spin.

The two Rowans, Athol and Eric, also came on the scene at this time, which leads me on to one of the most amusing tales I have heard from a Test cricketer. The man concerned is Eric Rowan, the batsman of the two brothers, and the incident was set off by a selection meeting which voted to leave him out of an upcoming Test. Strangely, this meeting had been convened during the previous Test, and Rowan still had to bat a second time after hearing he had been dropped.

As I have since discovered, Eric is not a man to keep his feelings secret. On this occasion, he publicly demonstrated his disgust by walking out to bat without gloves or 'box'. He scored a brilliant century, fired by defiance, but saved his most vivid gesture to the end.

The ground concerned has a pavilion behind the bowler's arm where the selectors were sitting, but the players have separate changing quarters square on. When Eric was out, he marched straight off down the wicket, arrived in front of the members' pavilion and gave a 'V' sign to the selectors before wheeling away to the dressing-rooms.

Another great character of this era was Jackie McGlew, who happens to be the first Test cricketer I ever met. I was on tour with my school in Natal when I was introduced to McGlew. Although he was a very small man, I remember being struck by his huge hands and thinking how their size explained his brilliance as a cover fielder.

McGlew will best be remembered, however, for his sticking qualities as a batsman. As England had 'Barnacle' Trevor Bailey, South Africa had McGlew to grind away the hours with unfailing concentration whenever his team was in need of a long innings.

Alan Melville, now a
cricket commentator,
produced a memorable
batting performance
during the famous
timeless Test in 1939
against England.

His most remarkable performance was against England at Trent Bridge in 1955 when he took five hours over 68 in the first innings and four hours over 51 in the second. Two years later, he beat Gibb's record for the slowest century in Test matches with a 545-minute ton against Australia.

McGlew had the misfortune to be captain of the 1960 team which toured England. I say misfortune, because it was a trip dogged with upsets and controversy all the way. The first signs of the strife over apartheid that was to come into contact with cricket arrived with the demonstrations that punctuated the trip. There was also the unpleasant saga of the no-balling of fast bowler Griffin for chucking, described elsewhere. To cap it all, the summer was wet and miserable and South Africa lost the series 3–0.

There was worse to come. In 1961–62, New Zealand went to

South Africa and had the cheek to take two Tests and share the rubber, chiefly due to the magnificent batting of John Reid. But this series was at least significant for the emergence of Peter Pollock, who was to become the country's finest fast bowler.

One man who missed the drawn series with New Zealand was Trevor Goddard, a man whom I hero-worshipped throughout my early years in South Africa. Goddard was still playing in the national side in 1970, by which time he was not far off his fortieth birthday. But during the late 'fifties and early 'sixties he was the great white chief of South African cricket, batting and bowling left-handed and fielding quite superbly close to the wicket. Figures can never completely encapsulate a man's worth to his side, but Goddard is well recommended by his performances: more than 2,500 Test runs at an average of 34.46 and 123 Test wickets, second only to Tayfield.

McGlew retired after the New Zealand series, and Goddard was voted in as captain–a decision that he quickly justified by holding the Australians to a 1–1 draw on their own territory in 1963–64, when in fact South Africa might well have won the final Test at Sydney and taken the series.

Peter Pollock was a star of that rubber. He was joined by two more who were to reach for glory and be denied it in full only by the political interference. Peter's brother, Graeme Pollock, and the sturdily-built all-rounder, Eddie Barlow, both appeared for the first time in 1963.

The Pollock brothers were idols throughout the latter part of the 'sixties. Peter, with his fair hair flailing behind him, was a fearsome sight as he ran into bowl–and far more so in 1969–70 when he had the equally awesome Procter at the other end. Graeme batted with a power and compulsion matched by few players that I have seen in my lifetime.

Graeme Pollock will be remembered for several marvellously uninhibited innings in England, for a stunning double-century against the 1969 Australians, and for some formidable contributions for the Rest of the World teams. But how much of the best of Pollock have we missed?

I played with both of the Pollock brothers during my brief spell with Eastern Province before coming to England, and I was helped in my development by them both, but notably by the elder and more senior Peter.

Barlow is something different again. I cannot help comparing myself with Eddie, because I don't think either of us were blessed with too much natural talent. But, just like me, he will fight every delivery to the death.

If South Africa were to begin Test cricket again immediately, Barlow would be the obvious choice as captain. Purely through his combatant nature, his irresistible will that defies anything to

beat him, I am sure he would be a great leader for his country.

By a strange coincidence, he has scored exactly the same number of runs for South Africa as Goddard—2,516. But in Barlow's case, the runs have come from 21 fewer innings and at a considerably improved average.

His worth as a bowler has often been underrated. Perhaps he is not exactly devastating, with his bustling approach and swinging style. But Barlow believes he is going to beat the bat with every ball—and that means a great deal.

There is a famous story that Barlow once approached Goddard, captain at the time, during a big partnership. He virtually

insisted on being given the ball, because he said he had a 'feeling' that he could break the stand. Goddard relented, and Barlow not only broke that partnership, he took two more wickets quickly. Ever since then, whenever Eddie feels like a bowl, he just swings his arms and tells the skipper he has got the feeling again.

Barlow is known as 'Bunter' to his cricketing friends, because until recently he wore some owlish glasses which, in combination with his stout figure, could comically liken him to the storybook English schoolboy character. But to the public of South Africa, Barlow was always known as 'God'. That led to a humorous confrontation on the last occasion that I played against him, because

Kenneth Bland, a talented batsman and remarkable fielder.

I had come back from Australia with the nickname 'The Messiah'!

South Africa now had the basis of the team that was to put them on the map, briefly but gloriously. Add to these four stars the likes of Bland, Lindsay, Richards and Procter and you have a magnificent machine capable of taking on and beating the best that the world could produce.

Bland's memory will live on and on, almost exclusively for his unbelievable fielding. The fact that he was an attractive and successful batsman, averaging just short of 50 from 39 Test innings, is scarcely taken into consideration. But perhaps that just magnifies the unrivalled talent of the man in the field. All I

103

Denis Lindsay makes a desperate attempt to run out Mike Smith during the second Test at Trent Bridge, 1965.

can say is that I have never seen anybody come close to his ability at cover – and I honestly don't expect to in my lifetime.

Denis Lindsay played only 19 Tests, but in that time he established a reputation as a marvellous wicketkeeper and, perhaps more important, a tremendous middle-order batsman. His finest hours came in the 1966–67 series against Australia under Peter Van der Merwe when he scored centuries in three of the five Tests.

As for Barry Richards and Mike Procter, I can add little to my comments at the start of this chapter. Richards is the finest batsman I have ever played against and Procter could claim world class both as batsman and bowler. I played with both of them in the South African schools sides and our careers have run almost parallel – apart, of course, from the fact that I have been far luckier in Test opportunities.

There can be no doubt that the side which demolished Australia in 1970 was the finest that South Africa has ever fielded.

Above right
Ali Bacher, a talented captain.

And the one man we have not mentioned, who did as much as anyone to make it so, is Ali Bacher.

Without ever ranking among the greatest cricketers his country has produced, Bacher rates alongside Frank Worrell in my book. Just as Worrell pulled the West Indian islands into one, so Bacher moulded the provincial rivalries of South Africa into one great unit, then captained it with a talent that few could have matched.

His word was gospel, and I can say quite happily that Ali Bacher, the cricket-player medical man, was one of the greatest men I have ever had the pleasure to meet.

So the pinnacle was reached, and this side was ready for a take-off into the realms of the immortals. Had they been able to stay together for two or three years, I feel they could have made out a strong case to be the number one team in Test history. Yes, they could have stood above them all – the 1948 Australians and the rest – just given the chance. Instead, South Africa is left with a future clouded with shadows and doubt.

New Zealand

New Zealand's left-handed batsman from the war to the mid 1960s, Bert Sutcliffe.

Below
J. Cowie, one of New Zealand's best bowlers, taking 114 wickets during the 1937 tour of England.

Whatever misfortunes are in store for New Zealand in years to come, nothing is likely to rival the disaster of their first morning in Test cricket.

With just a few overs bowled of their debut Test against England at Christchurch in 1930, New Zealand's score stood at a humiliating 21 for seven. All credit to them for not giving up Test cricket as a bad job, there and then.

In the years that have followed, New Zealand have rarely hit any great heights of success. Although they are a country of great sporting traditions, based especially on the triumphs of the All Blacks rugby team, their cricket has never possessed the depth to sustain a genuine challenge to the world's best.

When MCC have toured New Zealand, I have noticed with surprise that we have played against the same nucleus of 18 or 20 players in almost every fixture. To me, this suggests a lack of foresight. The young talent is simply not being given an airing.

I am afraid the game is not promoted as it should be in New Zealand. Although they have been offered the opportunity to accept individual tours, at least from MCC, they have recently preferred to stay in the shelter, taking in the major countries only after they have completed an exhausting tour of Australia.

These short, wind-down tours are bound to be an anti-climax. New Zealand has much to offer, but their progress is certain to be stilted until they do all in their power to push for separate tours. After the big crowds and the tension of Australia, New Zealand will inevitably suffer by comparison. Their crowds never see foreign opposition at its best – if individual tours could be arranged, the interest would be so much greater.

Back on that January morning in 1930, however, New Zealand's cricketers were probably wishing England had not bothered to come out at all. Tom Lowry, who had spent three years in England playing for Cambridge University and Somerset, won his first toss as New Zealand captain and chose to bat in conditions that turned out to be ideal for the England seamers.

Things were bleak enough when Nichols claimed the first three wickets while the score crept to 15. But, at 21, Maurice Allom,

Martin Donnelly, who also batted for Oxford, Middlesex and Warwickshire.

then of Surrey and later to become a President of MCC, delivered one of the most devastating overs the game has seen.

The first ball was edged for one, the second claimed a wicket, the third was blank. Allom then performed the hat-trick with his remaining three deliveries to finish the over with four wickets in five balls and leave New Zealand in that drunken state of 21 for seven.

Fortunately for their spirit, the tailenders took the total into three figures, and although England eventually won comfortably by eight wickets, New Zealand performed far more capably in the Tests which followed and claimed three draws.

Within 18 months, New Zealand were in England for their first recognised international at Lord's. It was the only Test scheduled for the tour, but the New Zealanders gave such a great show that two more were hurriedly tagged on to the end of the programme. Having faced a first-innings deficit of more than 200, New Zealand scored 469 for nine at the second attempt and then whipped out half the England side for 144 before the game ended in a well-balanced draw.

England recovered her pride and composure to win the next Test by an innings, and the last, at Manchester, was completely wrecked by the weather. In looking up the records of this series, I was amused to note a reference to the infamous Manchester weather. Even today, Englishmen tend to think that it always rains in Manchester, and it seems that things were no different 45 years ago. Apparently, the weather was consistently bad for most Old Trafford Tests up to the Second World War. The only two Tests abandoned without a ball bowled up to that time were both at Manchester, and of 10 drawn Tests on the ground, seven were affected by weather! On this particular occasion, the first two days were completely washed out, and only three hours play was possible on the third and final day.

Around this time, New Zealand's bowling relied heavily on a seamer named Cowie. He played only nine Tests, but took 45 wickets. In 1937, he collected 114 victims at under 20 runs apiece on the New Zealand tour of England – and in the first Test at Lord's he dismissed a certain young English opener making his Test debut for nought and 1. His name? Len Hutton.

Australia paid their first official visit to their neighbouring country immediately after the Second World War, and inflicted one of the heaviest defeats imaginable at the first attempt. The only Test of the tour was played at Wellington and Australia, probably eager to assert their authority, fielded a formidable bowling attack that included Lindwall, Miller and the spinners Toshack and O'Reilly.

The wicket was affected by rain and although Lindwall claimed only one scalp with the new ball, the advent of the

Opposite
John Reid led New Zealand to her first Test success, against the West Indies in 1956.

108

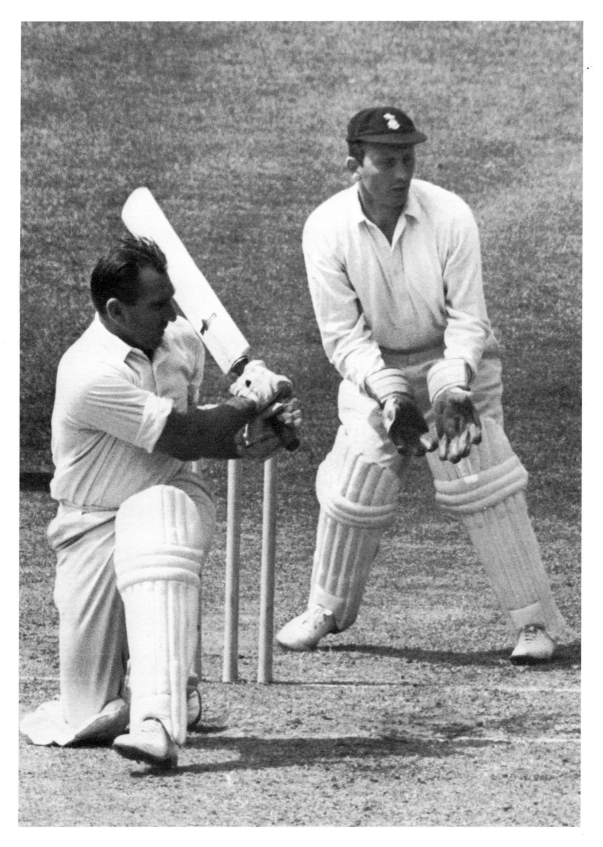

spinners put New Zealand in utter confusion. From 37 for two they plunged to 42 all out, Bill O'Reilly taking five for 14 and Toshack, four for 12.

Australia managed only 199 for nine before declaring, that man Cowie picking up six cheap wickets, but New Zealand's batting was just as abysmal in the second innings. Again, they looked set to achieve at least respect at 36 for three, but the last seven wickets fell for 18 and Australia went home smugly, with victory by an innings and 103 runs.

In the ensuing years, Australia sent understrength teams to New Zealand, and there were no further Tests between them until 1973–74, when three Tests were played in each country. Ian Chappell's Aussies won their home series 2–0, but Bevan Congdon, rallying his men as only he could, produced a memorable win over their closest enemy in the second leg of the rubber, which was tied 1–1.

Meanwhile, New Zealand had improved sufficiently from that 1946 drubbing to send a useful party to England three years later. All four Tests were drawn, and three of the finest cricketers New Zealand has produced were introduced to the English public.

Two of them were left-handers, the opener Bert Sutcliffe and a middle-order man, Martin Donnelly. Sadly for New Zealand, Donnelly played only seven Tests before retiring, his career savaged by the war years. But in the first three Tests in 1949, his scores read 64, 206, 75 and 80. He also played for Oxford, Middlesex and Warwickshire, scoring almost 10,000 runs in his career.

If Donnelly departed all too quickly, Sutcliffe's life at the top was extraordinarily lengthy. He played his first Test in 1946, and bowed out after the tour of India and Pakistan in 1965, by which time he was 42. In all, he played 42 Tests and averaged 40. His run aggregate for his country has been exceeded only by Congdon and the other great New Zealand character to emerge in 1949, John Reid.

Reid was introduced in the third Test at Manchester – where it didn't rain for once – and set the pattern for his international career with a half-century in his debut innings. Making a rather less auspicious start to a Test career on England's side was Brian Close, then only 18 and out for nought.

I've already talked of the idols that I worshipped through my schooldays in South Africa and the heroes that I still retain today. John Reid can be added to that list.

In 1961, when I was at college in Queenstown, Reid led the New Zealanders on a five-Test tour of South Africa. I was immediately struck by the appearance of the man. He looked as strong as an ox, and his batting proved it. To me, he is a man apart as far as New Zealand are concerned. He carried the teams

Opposite
Bevan Congdon, a captain New Zealand are finding difficult to replace.

110

of the early 1960s, bowling useful seamers and scoring more runs than anybody else. When he retired in 1965 after 58 Tests, New Zealand lost a general.

It was Reid who led New Zealand to her first success in the Test arena—a home win over the West Indies in 1956. Six years later, on the tour that I watched in South Africa, New Zealand startled the cricket world by winning two Tests and sharing the series. Although Dick Motz took 81 wickets on the tour, Reid was the shining light. His 1,915 runs in 30 innings eclipsed the record aggregate for a South African tour.

After one series under Barry Sinclair, the New Zealand captaincy passed to Graham Dowling, who achieved Test wins over India in successive series, and a 1–0 triumph in a three-match rubber in Pakistan in 1969–70.

Congdon took over in 1972, and even apart from the momentous win over Australia under his command, I believe his influence on New Zealand cricket has been massive. Bev was a true cricket fighter in the same mould as South Africa's Eddie Barlow.

I shall never forget his bravery in the Nottingham Test of 1973. Ray Illingworth had set New Zealand what everyone thought was an impossible target—no team batting fourth had ever made 479 runs to win a match. But Congdon came out to bat in a mood of sheer determination. John Snow hit him on the jaw with a short ball, but he stayed on and battled to a magnificent 176. His team failed to win, but they scared us all by scoring 440, a score certainly inspired by the attitude of their captain.

Perhaps New Zealanders did not realise how much Bevan Congdon meant to their cricket until he had gone. They have still not satisfactorily replaced him.

Their most recent captain has been Glenn Turner, a man who looked destined for immortality when he first burst onto the international scene. A grafter in his early Test match days, Turner eventually developed into a more complete player. But, despite a decade at the top of the order for Worcestershire and for his country, he has never quite realised the hopes that so many people had for him.

Turner was sorted out by the bouncers, as so many leading batsmen of recent years have been. Now he is a big fish in a small pool—a pool that will never grow into a lake until New Zealand's cricket people, from the top administrators down to the players, achieve the drive and ambition of their All Blacks rugby counterparts.

Pakistan

Fazal Mahmood
returning to the pavilion
after a brilliant day's
bowling during the 1954
Oval Test against
England.

Test cricket may have come of age after 100 years, but Pakistan, by far the youngest of its offspring, is scarcely out of the pram stage. It is barely a quarter of a century since this country, formed from the partition of India, blazed onto the Test scene with a series of spectacular triumphs.

Lean years followed but, as I write, Pakistan possess the strongest squad they have ever fielded. It is a pity, however, that the performances of their modern team on the field will inevitably be scarred by the wounds of the conflict which preceded the 1976–77 series in Australia.

Their captaincy had changed with baffling frequency during recent years, and the obvious undercurrent of unrest was brought to a head by the players' demands for better terms after their 1976 victory over New Zealand. Led by captain Mushtaq Mohammad, most of the senior players stressed that they would only be available for the Australian trip if their demands were met. Sadly, the whole matter was dragged into the open, and the newspapers understandably thrived on it.

Mushtaq was sacked as captain and four other players were ordered to appear before the national cricket board. The saga continued with an amazing turnabout, the selectors being sacked, a new panel being nominated and Mushtaq being reinstated.

It was a sad business and, whatever the merits of either side, it merely served to harden my conviction that dirty washing such as this should be kept private. Situations over money can always crop up at national level as well as in the countries and clubs. But they should be solved by both parties sitting round a table and thrashing out a compromise long before they get near the pages of a newspaper.

With all that said, it is satisfying to see Pakistan thriving, because they are now an attractive team–which can only be good for the game. In batsmen such as Mushtaq, Majid Khan, Zaheer Abbas and Asif Iqbal, they have players of grace and flair who love to attack the bowling. If they get to the top, and seriously threaten the current dominance of Australia, the West Indies and,

to a lesser extent at present, England, they will have done it by being aggressive.

They have a player in Javed Miandad who could become one of the most stunning young Test stars of recent times. Sussex spotted him during the 1975 World Cup in England, and he signed a contract with the county in 1976. By the end of that season, he had already displayed his fabulous potential with some magnificent innings, notably a century which took us to victory over Hampshire.

He bowls leg-breaks with developing skill, fields brilliantly, and seems to me to have only one drawback–he can barely speak any English. When he first came to Sussex, we had to conduct any conversations with Javed via an interpreter–normally his great friend, Sadiq Mohammad.

Throughout their time in Test cricket, Pakistan have made a habit of unveiling talent at a younger age than any other country. The four youngest players ever to appear in Tests are all Pakistanis, and Wisden informs me that of the youngest 20, 11 came from Pakistan.

Mushtaq is easily the baby of the party. He made his Test debut at a precocious 15 years and 124 days in the 1958–59 series against the West Indies, and has been virtually an automatic choice ever since.

Before Mushtaq came his famous brother, the little master Hanif. At the age of 17, Hanif Mohammad opened the batting for Pakistan in their inaugural Test match–a disastrous debut against their neighbours, India. Hanif made 51 in the first innings, but Pakistan were beaten by an innings. Revenge came swiftly with a victory by a similar margin in the second Test, but India won the series.

Hanif went on to play 55 Test matches, still a Pakistan record. He scored almost 4,000 runs at an average of more than 40 and was made famous by his completely unhurried style and his deadpan expression. In the 1957–58 series against the West Indies, he stayed almost three days for 337–the longest recorded innings in first-class cricket. Hanif still holds the record individual score in any country–499 for Karachi in 1959, when he was run out going for his 500th run from the last ball of the day.

In their early days, Pakistan used matting on their home pitches. The effect was quite startling. Fazal Mahmood, Pakistan's opening bowler for 10 years and still their highest wicket-taker, had the ability to cut the ball away off matting as though he was bowling leg-breaks at a great pace. Keith Miller of Australia tells a story that, in 1956, he once faced the first five balls of an over from Fazal and groped at each one as it fizzed away. The sixth broke back off the mat and bowled him.

The mats could provide part of the explanation for Pakistan's

Two of Pakistan's leading batsmen: Mushtaq Mohammad (left) and Zaheer Abbas.

Right
**Javed Miandad,
Pakistan's rising Test
star.**

early success, during which they won series against England,
Australia and the West Indies. The Australians certainly con-
sidered it a major contribution to their 1956 embarrassment at
Karachi when they were bowled out for 80 by Fazal.

Richie Benaud did not forget that match, and when Australia
returned to Pakistan two years later, he set out to 'put things
right'. The Aussies thrashed Pakistan on turf in the new Lahore
ground, and when the mat was rolled out for the next Test at
Karachi, Benaud was ready.

During the introduction of teams, Benaud whispered in the ear
of Pakistani President Ayub Khan that his country could only
reach cricket's top flight if she began to use turf pitches everywhere. The comment had the desired effect, and by the start of
the 1960s, grass was taking over. The adjustments that this change
necessitated meant that Pakistan were not a force for the next 15
years; the World Cup of 1975 announced their return to power.

Their future, at least for the next few years, is an exciting one,
because they provide a blend of the best qualities. If I had to
describe a Pakistani cricketer to a Martian, I would liken him to a
cross between an Indian and a West Indian. Spin is still important
in Pakistan, as in India, but their batsmen play with the same
joyful freedom as the West Indians.

Left
**Hanif Mohammad,
Mushtaq's famous
brother who set a
number of batting
records during his long
Test career.**

Pakistan's history as yet is brief, and recently it has become
clustered with unwanted controversy. If they can clear the decks
for an exhibition of their true talent, and keep the rows to themselves, I feel we are in for increasing competition from them in
years to come.

119

Rows and Riots

I throw down my bat in anger after a high ball from Holding during the second Test at Lord's, 1976.

Below
Lord Harris, MCC captain during the 1879 Australian tour which was notable for the first recorded walk-off and crowd riot.

Lords, nobles and gentlemen put cricket on the road. It was created for the well bred and it initially existed for a serene, if sometimes pompous, public. But troubled times were not far away when Charles Bannerman received the first delivery of the inaugural Test from Alfred Shaw at Melbourne in 1877.

Just two years later, on England's second official trip to Australia, controversy erupted in a pre-Test fixture at Sydney. Gregory, the captain of New South Wales, rushed onto the field to argue with the umpires over an lbw decision. Looking back now, his manner seems quite comical when one recalls the dignity associated with that age.

Lord Harris, who was skippering MCC, was apparently asked to authorise a change of umpires. Understandably he refused, and Gregory marched his batsmen to the pavilion in what must be the first walk-off in the history of the first-class game.

What happened next constituted the first recorded cricket crowd disturbance of any note. The incensed New South Wales supporters rushed the pitch and threatened the MCC team. Lord Harris was apparently attacked by a chap brandishing a stick and the incident led to a rift in international cricket relations, just as they were beginning to grow.

As a measure of MCC's disapproval, no Test match was included on the Australian itinerary for their visit to England the following summer. One was eventually arranged – in September! – but this episode seems to stand as the earliest forerunner to the events I shall relate in this section – the rows and riots of Test cricket.

It would be quite wrong to expect that a game of such physical output and high level of mental application will not occasionally produce a flashpoint. Players' tempers can flare under pressure, an enraged crowd sometimes cannot withhold their emotions, the cunning plan of a team or individual can lead to bad feeling and inquests.

Modern, less inhibited times have unquestionably accelerated the chain of Test match disturbances. But my first dip into the files of the angry Tests dates back 35 years, to Larwood and Voce, Jardine and Woodfull – the notorious 'bodyline' tour of 1932–33.

Woodfull ducks under a ball from Larwood during the infamous 'bodyline' tour of Australia in 1932–33.

Bodyline

There is no chapter in cricket history quite as compelling as England's tour of Australia in the winter of 1932–33. This is the series that came to be known as the bodyline war. It reads like a thriller serial and its repercussions can still be felt to this day.

To explain first the term, 'bodyline' is the word which was coined at the time to explain the England tactic of employing their pace bowlers, chiefly Harold Larwood, to bowl fast, short balls aimed at the batsman's body. It sounds simple enough, but the furore caused by the experiment was devastating.

I have to say at the outset that I find the concept fascinating. The drama and controversy which surrounded the series has never since been emulated; if I pick up a cricket book these days, I always look first for any account of 'bodyline'.

The first thing a police investigation must look for is the motive of any suspect in a crime case. Likewise, whether or not bodyline is considered 'criminal', the reasons behind its use must be examined initially.

Number one motive can be explained in two words – Don Bradman. To anyone English, Bradman's phenomenal run-scoring was simply getting out of hand. Douglas Jardine, the MCC skipper, no doubt spent most of his waking hours turning over various schemes to stall this prolific man; bodyline arrived as a godsend.

'Gubby' Allen was in the England side throughout the series, bowling either as Larwood's opening partner or as first change. It is said that he, above all others, disapproved of the tactic and refused to be part of it. Yet when I have talked to him on the topic in recent years, he insists that the 'plan' was not formulated before the team had arrived in Australia.

I have been interested enough in this subject to conduct my own enquiries, and from what I can gather, bodyline was born when an anonymous MCC member noticed the great Bradman flinch when delivered a short, rising ball. This player told Jardine about his hunch and so the idea germinated.

Bradman missed the first Test through illness and England subsequently won. He played in the second and squared it at 1–1 through a superb, unbeaten century on an uncomfortable Melbourne wicket. Then came the third Test at Adelaide, the match described by Wisden's correspondent as 'probably the most unpleasant ever played'.

Woodfall, the Australian captain, took a battering around the body from Larwood, and wicketkeeper Bertie Oldfield was felled by a blow to the head while trying to hook a bouncer. Larwood later admitted in his own book on the episode that he thought Oldfield was dead; thankfully, the ball had missed the vulnerable temple and struck a thicker part of the skull.

Now the crowd, already angered by the system, began to chant obscenely and I can imagine that, in this instance, real fear crept into some English hearts. But fear was not absent from the Australian players, either, and England's attack was a success in as much that they won by a staggering 338 runs.

Woodfull is reported to have commented to England manager Pelham Warner (later Sir Pelham) during the assault that: 'There are two sides out there. One is playing cricket and the other is not. The game is too good to be spoilt. It is time some people got out of the game.'

Apparently, both the disputed deliveries – at Woodfull and Oldfield – pitched outside the off stump and were not related to the bodyline theory apart from the fact that they were bowled to intimidate. But now the action was speeding off the field, with the drafting of the most famous telegram in the history of the game. It came from the Australian Board of Control, it was aimed at the desk of the MCC secretary 11,000 miles away at Lord's and it read:—

Above
Woodfull, the Australian captain during the bodyline series.

Above centre
Wicketkeeper Bertie Oldfield as a batsman. He received a blow to the head from Larwood.

Above right
Harold Larwood, whose technique during the 1932–33 tour eventually led to bowling aimed at the body being banned.

Bodyline bowling has assumed such proportions as to menace the best interests of the game, making protection of the body by the batsmen the main consideration. This is causing intensely bitter feeling between the players as well as injury. In our opinion it is unsportsmanlike. Unless stopped at once it is likely to upset the friendly relations existing between Australia and England.

The cable struck home like a right hook from Muhammad Ali. Up to this point, the MCC, cut off from an authentic picture of events, had probably not been aware of the magnitude of the incident. Now, wheels were set in motion, film was flown in from Australia, and a reply was drafted:

We, Marylebone Cricket Club, deplore your cable. We deprecate your opinion that there has been unsportsmanlike play. We have fullest confidence in captain, team and managers and are convinced that they would do nothing to infringe either the laws of cricket or the spirit of the game. We have no evidence that our confidence has been misplaced. Much as we regret accidents to Woodfull and Ponsford, we understand that in neither case was the bowler to blame.

If the Australian Board of Control wish to propose a new law or rule, it shall receive our careful consideration in due course.

We hope the situation is not now as serious as your cable would seem to indicate, but if it is such as to jeopardise the good relations between English and Australian cricketers and you consider it desirable to cancel remainder of programme we would consent, but with great reluctance.

Faced with an offer to cancel the tour, the ball was back in Australia's court. Under Jardine's insistence, the insinuation that his theory was unsportsmanlike was withdrawn and the remaining Tests were played in comparative peace, England winning them both to take the series 4–1.

I cannot find Jardine guilty of a cricket crime, simply because if I look myself in the eye and ask what I would have done in the same circumstances, I confess I would have been tempted to adopt his plan.

It was the only way to stop Bradman – and how it succeeded! His average at the end of the series was 56.57, still impressive for any mortal but way below his efforts in the previous series against England, in which he averaged 139.14.

Don't forget Australia had one or two others who could bat a bit. Ponsford, who averaged 55 in the previous series, was cut to 23, and skipper Woodfull's average slumped from 57 to 33. Whether England could have won without the use of bodyline is a question that will never be answered. All that remains is the aftermath – and that in itself played a substantial part in the reshaping of the game.

Intimidation by means of persistent bowling aimed at the body was eventually outlawed. Rules governing limitation of fielders behind square on the leg side were introduced to render short-pitched bowling less effective in the absence of a ring of catchers.

In this light, it must be said that bodyline did some good. The game has been improved by these rule changes and one would think that a repetition of bodyline is now impossible. But here, I have to dissent, for I believe I have been through bodyline in recent years.

It is my opinion that Dennis Lillee and Jeff Thomson operated a similar system when MCC toured Australia in 1974–75. Yet it passed unnoticed. Any use of excess bouncers designed to scare a batsman – and this still goes on with alarming frequency – could be classed as bodyline.

Facts of life dictate that the 1932–33 season will always be remembered with a sour taste, disregarding the skill which surely appeared during the series. All that is left is theories, unanswered questions, and some remarkable anecdotes.

What would have occurred if the episode had split England and Australia? Would we still not be on speaking terms now? Why didn't the umpires intervene to curb any dangerous bowling? How much effect did the inconsistent bounce of the wickets have on the affair? Just how cool was Jardine as he strode arrogantly out to open England's innings at Adelaide, the crowd hooting at him and his outrageous Harlequin cap – worn as a sign of pure defiance? Or as he marched from the ground to the hotel, refusing offers of a lift for his own safety?

Douglas Jardine, the MCC captain who implemented the bodyline theory.

Even now, some Australians are reluctant to talk about the issue. It still rankles that painfully. When I visited Sir Donald Bradman, one of the nicest people I have ever met, he refused to throw any mud. But his wife was more eager to talk and she gave me a story more significant than most.

When the affair was reaching its hostile peak, Bill Ponsford decided he needed more than the regular protection. So Lady Bradman set about the task, making him protectors for his chest, stomach and arms. In her words, 'He went out to bat looking like a Michelin man'.

Throwing

If the name Mabarak Ali means absolutely nothing to you, I am sure you are not alone. I, too, had never heard of this gentlemen until I discovered he is the holder of an odd distinction – he has been no-balled for chucking, 30 times in one innings.

Mr Ali was performing for Trinidad against Barbados in 1941–42 when the incident occurred. Yet, despite his unparalleled feat, the names of Ernest Jones, Tony Lock, Geoff Griffin and Ian Meckiff will be recognised by many more. For these are

the only bowlers to have been called for throwing in Test cricket.

Sir Donald Bradman probably described the throwing problem most neatly in his widely reported quote of 1960: 'It is the most complex question I have ever known in cricket, because it is not a matter of fact, but of opinion and interpretation. It is so involved that two men of equal goodwill and sincerity could take opposite views.'

The crux of the problem to which Sir Donald was referring is, of course, obtaining concrete proof that a bowler is unfair according to the laws – meaning that when he delivers the ball, his arm is bent at the elbow. Detecting a chuck with the naked eye is fraught with difficulties and for this reason it was not until the advent of slow-motion film that the campaign to rid the game of throwers got seriously underway.

That is not to say the problem did not always exist beneath the surface. Indeed, before the turn of the century, there was plenty of verbal crossfire on the subject, culminating in the no-balling of Australia's Jones during the 1897–98 series against England.

More than 56 years passed before the next case of a Test call. This time it was Tony Lock, playing against the West Indies in

Jamaica in 1954. Four years later, it was the turn of Australia's Meckiff to come under suspicion – and here, press influence was brought to bear.

When Meckiff bowled for Australia against MCC in the 1958–59 tour, he was the subject of a lot of criticism and direct inferences that he chucked. The hint was not overlooked, underlining my conviction that the media play a huge part in this subject. Once they have cast doubts, umpires must feel more comfortable about calling the bowler.

Meckiff's career subsequently ended sadly. He was no-balled for throwing four times in his opening over of Australia's first Test again South Africa in 1963–64 and immediately taken off for the match, after which he retired from the game.

In 1960 there was the case of Griffin, the young South African bowler, who apparently had a naturally bent arm anyway. He was called five times on the opening day of the Lord's Test – the first man to be no-balled for chucking in a Test in England – yet on the second day he became the first South African to perform a hat-trick in Test cricket. Further calls followed, and in an exhibition match after the premature finish of the Test, he was no-balled four times in an over. Ironically, he finished the over bowling underarm and was called again for not notifying the umpire of a change in action!

The Meckiff affair prompted the Imperial Cricket Conference to issue stricter directives to umpires, but much unwanted drama has since been taken out of the issue by the regulation that suspect bowlers should first be reported and filmed rather than called.

Danger is obviously associated with throwing when it relates to a quick bowler, because a flick from the elbow can double his pace and make the illegal ball quite unplayable – I have seen it happen during Tests in England and I can tell you it was not pleasant for the batsman. The men who throw all the time are not so deadly because one can adjust to their regular rhythm; it's the man who pulls one out of the bag at you that can cause disaster.

Spinners are not exempt from the laws and I believe orthodox spinners very often chuck, simply through the nature of their action. I have faced and watched the gentlest orthodox slow bowlers throwing quite blatantly without any hint of action against them.

A slow throw will not kill you, however – and it is the threat of someone being killed or maimed by a bent elbow that causes the concern – and probably always will.

Beamers and Bouncers

Two beamers have been directed at me in a career of more than 50 Tests; in that time I have certainly faced more than 200

bouncers. Yet, without hesitation, I would go through another 200 short-pitched balls to avoid another two head-high rockets.

Both types of delivery are a problem of contemporary cricket, but while the bouncer, in limited numbers, is an acceptable part of a fast bowler's armoury, the beamer is absolutely taboo.

At Test standard, I am not prepared to accept any excuse at all for the bowling of a beamer. The usual plea is that the ball slipped but my view is that if a fellow is good enough to be picked to bowl for his country, he should not have too much trouble in hitting the pitch.

On each occasion that I was subjected to this ordeal, the bowler concerned was clearly agitated. The first was Sarfraz Nawaz of Pakistan. His anger was aroused when my batting partner twice halted him in his run-up because someone was moving behind the arm. 'Sarf' took out his frustration with two beamers. The first, at my partner, was inaccurate. The second, at me, was fast, furious and far too close for comfort.

Then, in the 1976 series against the West Indies, I came in to bat at Lord's to my customary noisy reception from the West Indian crowd. The atmosphere among the spectators was always transferred to the players and I swear they bowled twice as fast at me sometimes. On this occasion, I hit Michael Holding back over his head for four. This fine young paceman then seemed to lose his cool and I saw nothing as the next ball shot past my head.

I was angry enough to throw my bat down and words were passed both on the field and afterwards. But whatever I may have thought, it can never be proved that the ball was deliberately aimed at my head.

I liken bowling beamers to a man who is perpetually ill. People may call him a fake and a hypochondriac but only one man knows if he is really hurt—and that is himself. Only Sarfraz and Holding know to this day whether their beamers bowled at me were a cold-blooded, deliberate slice of their wrath, or whether they really were a slip of the hand.

There are few recorded cases of beamer controversies in Test history. I hope there will be even fewer in the future. I believe that any beamer, judged as a ball passing the batsman around or above head height, should be penalised by the addition of six runs. But that is a minor issue compared with the potential tragedy if such deliveries continue.

My fears on this count also apply to the subject of bumpers. Unfortunately, although I pray it will never come to it, urgent action may foolishly be postponed until a batsman is dead and buried in a Test arena.

Bouncers are the game's biggest worry because they occur in such vast numbers, particularly in recent series with the advent

of a new band of lightning fast bowlers in Dennis Lillee, Jeff Thomson, Andy Roberts, Michael Holding and Wayne Daniel. I have faced them all, but if I had to go through the mill against short-pitched intimidation again I would go out to bat wearing a helmet to protect my head.

There is no batsman in the world who enjoys such an assault. I want to go on living, and against men who fire at almost 100 miles per hour, it only takes a moment's lapse, a movement in the crowd or simply an unplayable bounce – and that could be my last ball in this world.

A bowler will adopt a bouncer attack for one of two reasons. He either wants to scare the batsman into surrendering his wicket or he is setting him up for an attempted hook and a catch. In moderation, neither method can be castigated; in excess, both should be drummed out of the game.

Intimidation can be sensed by players on the field and, if players are able to perceive the bowler's intention, the umpire should also be in on the act. Umpires cannot, of course, carry the

133

Zaheer Abbas on his way
to 240 for Pakistan
against England at The
Oval, 1974.

Above
Karachi, 7 March 1969: demonstrators holding up the match.

Left
Asif Iqbal of Pakistan, one of the world's best all-rounders.

can for any bouncer war – but I do feel that their directions should be stricter. Too many warnings are issued. One is enough – after that the offending bowler should be removed for the rest of the innings.

Many legitimate dismissals have been gained by the short-pitched ball, even in my Test experience. I remember both Geoff Boycott and John Jameson being teed up for the kill by the West Indies in 1973. Here were two batsmen renowned for their willingness to hook. The West Indian quick bowlers obligingly served up the bait – and both Boycott and Jameson swallowed it, offering up catches as the ball hurried on, causing them to mistime the shot.

I had the great satisfaction of trapping Australia's captain Ian Chappell in a similar way at Manchester in 1972. It was the first ball I had bowled to him, I dropped it short and he hooked, powerfully but straight to my man on the fence.

But I have also seen Test players clearly frightened by short-pitched bowling. It can happen with exaggerated effect when the wicket produces an unpredictable bounce. At Sydney, on MCC's 1974–75 tour, I faced two successive short balls. To the first, I was back and across and played it down off the splice of the bat. The next ball seemed to pitch around the same area, so I made the same movements, only for the ball to fly above my head, clear wicketkeeper Rod Marsh's leap and disappear to the boundary. When I walked down the wicket to examine the spot, I found that the two deliveries had marked the pitch less than half-an-inch apart. I defy any batsman in the world to counter that!

Eccentric wickets have certainly contributed to the tendency for more bouncers to be bowled per match. Another factor must be the greater financial incentives these days. Although I am a benefactor of the new rewards available for top-line cricketers, I still think that the attitude of the old-time amateurs was to be admired. They played with flair and adventure, they enjoyed themselves – and there was far less aggro.

Karachi, 8 March 1969: players run for safety as the pitch is invaded.

Crowds

1 March 1954 ... Georgetown, Guyana ... West Indian fans hurled bottles and beercans onto the field when local hero Clifford McWatt was adjudged run out for 98. England captain Len Hutton insisted the match went on.

30 Jan 1960 ... Port of Spain, Trinidad ... Crowd rioted after West Indian batting failure against England. Thousands invaded the pitch and the players were driven off.

New Year's Day 1966 ... Calcutta ... Overcrowding sparked crowd trouble before play could begin on second day of India v West Indies. Police battled with fans, the players were evacuated by cars, fires blazed on and off the field, wrecking stands.

12 February 1968 ... Kingston, Jamaica ... Police used tear-gas to quell the anger of a crowd incensed at the dismissal of Basil Butcher. Thousands stampeded in panic but all escaped with their lives. Brian Close carried two petrified women clear.

Calcutta, 17 December 1969: the match being delayed by enthusiasts on the pitch.

Terry Jenner collapses at the wicket after receiving a blow to the head by a ball from John Snow, Sydney, 1971.

8 March 1969 . . . Karachi . . . Student riots forced an abandonment on the third day—the first time a Test had been ended by crowd trouble in 650 matches, 452 of them featuring the opponents in this case, England.

16 December 1969 . . . Calcutta . . . Six people killed and 100 injured in mob riot outside the ground. More than 20,000 had queued up all night for the 8,000 remaining tickets. Those who failed clashed with buyers and police; many were trampled underfoot. The teams' hotel was stoned, and Australian captain Bill Lawry was later involved in an incident with a photographer as the Indian crowd threw stones.

These are just a sordid selection of crowd disturbances affecting Test cricket. All of them occurred in the last 25 years, but as I recalled at the start of this section, crowd trouble dates right back to 1879.

There are various ways in which outsiders from the general public can interfere with a cricket match – and there are numerous reasons for their actions. Primarily, however, I believe it is down to the players to set an example by their behaviour. It will not solve the problem, but it will certainly ease tension in high-pressure moments such as a disputed dismissal. If a crowd sees one of their idols show annoyance at the decision, they will support him. And in many cases, the support has stretched far beyond the vocal chords.

Troublemakers are invariable confined to an isolated few, whose passion may be stirred by alcohol, politics or just an overgrown sense of patriotism. These men can easily incite those around them, particularly in the packed and excitable crowds of the West Indies, India and Pakistan.

Once, while playing in South Africa, I was 'out' caught behind four times in an innings. Each time, the umpire gave me not out. Three times I stayed, but on the fourth occasion I walked. Now if that had happened during a Test on foreign soil, all hell could have broken loose, and the umpire, as well as myself, would have been a target.

Umpires have a thankless task in grounds such as the cauldron of Calcutta. With 80,000 people screaming, how can he possibly hear a nick for a bat-pad catch? But if the local bowler has his appeal rejected, the crowd will waste no time before showing their anger. Before anyone can restore order the stand could be burning down.

The political riots are led by spectators who are not in the ground to watch cricket at all. Test matches are the biggest public gatherings in India and Pakistan and so provide an ideal platform for the disgruntled student leaders to demonstrate their feelings. The fact that these riots normally coincide with a controversial moment is incidental – the students are merely waiting for an excuse.

One fairly unique case was that of the 'Free George Davis' demonstrators at Headingley in 1975. They struck in the middle of the night, sabotaging the wicket with knives, forks and oil, forcing the sensational abandonment of the England–Australia Test.

Perhaps, once, the protesters would simply have waved banners and shouted outside 10 Downing Street. But, now, such occurrences are commonplace. By halting a Test match – and depriving millions of people of their expected entertainment, they hit the front page of every newspaper and win the sought-after television interviews. One of their number was jailed for the incident. But George Davis was eventually freed. . .

My dread is that, one day, all Test grounds around the world will have high fences to keep fans off the pitch. I fervently hope that situation does not arise because I am one of a huge proportion of Test players who hate having to perform in a cage.

Isolated occasions of one or two spectators encroaching on the field can be really amusing – remember the streaker at Lord's in 1975? One of the sights in Test cricket which I appreciate most is seeing hundreds of children staging their own mini-matches during the intervals, while their elders stretch their legs and take a peep at the pitch. All this would be lost if the fences arrived.

I always stress that the game is only as good as the players, but I admit my thoughts are slightly clouded on one of the most famous crowd issues of Test history. It happened at Sydney in February 1971, the last of the six-Test series, in which Ray Illingworth led England to a glorious 2–0 win and recaptured The Ashes from Australian soil for the first time in 38 years.

When Terry Jenner ducked into a short ball from John Snow and lay poleaxed on the pitch, the stadium erupted into venomous boos. Umpire Rowan warned Snow for intimidation and both Snow and his captain Illingworth returned fire, angrily claiming that it was the first bouncer he had bowled in the over.

Flashpoint arrived when Snow walked down to his customary fielding position at fine leg. Amid the thunderous din of disapproval, Snow's arm was grabbed by a man in the crowd, who, most reports indicate, was much the worse for drink. When Snow pulled away angrily and walked in 15 yards, beer cans rained onto the ground around him. His team-mate Bob Willis ran down to the corner to help, but only succeeded in antagonising the crowd still further. Then Illingworth ran over, kicked a couple of cans away and abruptly led his team off the field.

Only seven minutes passed before the England team reappeared and resumed the match. But it had been enough to cause a major stir. Well, was Illingworth right? My first observation is that he clearly could not put his fielders – or at least a fielder – where he wanted to. The situation was interfering with his position as fielding captain and, as such, the cans had to stop. When he took the action, drastic though it may have been, the cans did stop. He was proved correct in his judgement.

If a different, more traditional man had been leading England, the team would probably have stayed on. But Illingworth was, and still is, a tough Yorkshireman. Being what he is, he just could not accept cricket in those conditions. People might say he should have avoided sending Snow to the voluble 'Hill' area of the ground. But why should he? The crowd are basically there to watch, not to interfere.

A spectator grabs John Snow after the Jenner incident.

Looking back on the affair in cold blood – an easy thing to do, I admit – I believe I would have adopted something of a compromise. I would like to think I'd have called my players into the centre of the field, stopped the action and given the authorities five minutes to placate the crowd and cool the fire. If that didn't happen, I would have done just as Ray Illingworth did, and lead my men off.

Crowds have played a leading part in Test cricket's century. Their role over the past 20 years or so has not always been that of the goodie, either. Too often, they have worn the black cloak of the villain. If things do not improve, security for the players, and the peaceable watchers, may have to be strengthened. But the day when fences are built around international arenas will be the day when, for me, cricket will never again be the same game.

Recent rows

John Snow and I have played a lot of cricket together, seen a lot of places together. We have also been involved in two of the most controversial incidents of recent Test history.

Snow, my team-mate with both Sussex and England, was dropped from the England side after allegedly barging India's Sunny Gavaskar to the ground during the 1969 series in England. But the incident raised a number of interesting points.

As Gavaskar set off for a short single, Snowy dashed to pick up the ball. Their paths crossed, and at the point of collision, John dropped his shoulder, knocking the little Indian to the ground. Now there is no doubt in my mind that John did bump Gavaskar and that what he did was wrong. But I cannot agree with those who said that the barge was vicious.

Both John and I have strong views on the topic of right-of-way. Just who does have priority when a batsman is scuttling down the wicket and the bowler needs to get round him to the ball for a run-out attempt? My view is that it should be the bowler, and I feel that Snow's action was chiefly a sign of frustration at being baulked as he went for the ball.

The culmination of the episode was that Snow picked up Gavaskar's bat and tossed it back to him. Again, there are those who claim he threw it AT the batsman – an assertion that I cannot agree with. Knowing John as I do, I feel I understand his actions and his motives. On this occasion, I believe he was just lobbing the bat back in a gesture of apology, ready to continue with the game.

Naturally enough, the clash was seized upon by the media. Television's slow-motion film whirred into action and the incident was flashed around the country on the evening news programmes. The following morning's papers were full of the story, some criticising Snow in heavily couched terms. The authorities stepped in and he was suspended for the next Test.

A chapter of my Test career that I long to forget, but am constantly reminded of, happened on the 1973–74 tour of the West Indies. It was the last ball of the day, Bernard Julien was giving it the dead bat and I moved up to my silly point position, very close, hoping to snap up a catch from his defensive prod.

At the time, I was not consciously aware that it was the last ball of the day, not aware of Alvin Kallicharran, the batsman at the non-striker's end, and any thought of running out Kalli was far from my head. But that is just what happened, sparking an ugly scene that could have caused a riot but for the authorities reinstating him the following morning.

Instead of dropping the ball down in front of him, as I had expected, Julien pushed it past me five or six yards towards cover. I turned and gave chase, thinking the batsmen might be running, and as I picked the ball up I noticed that Kallicharran was out of his ground. Only as my eager throw shattered the stumps at the non-striker's end did I realise that Kalli had his gloves off and was following the already retreating Julien back to the pavilion.

John Snow colliding with Gavaskar, Lord's, 27 July 1971.

The umpire had no doubts, however, raising his finger instantly. What followed was unpleasant for me, but not half as unpleasant as it might have been if Kallicharran's dismissal had stood. In my defence, I have to say that I honestly thought the batsmen could be running; with my back to the wicket I could not have known that they had set off for the dressing-room. I must also reiterate my opinion that Alvin was very silly to leave his crease while the ball was still technically in play.

If the same set of circumstances were to occur again, knowing what I do now, I would probably check myself and avoid a repetition. But next time, I suppose, it will be something different.

In the cold light of day, when the heat is off, retractions are easy. Maybe Douglas Jardine wishes he had not invented body-line, maybe Sarfraz and Holding regret the beamers they bowled at me, maybe John Snow is sorry he knocked down Sunny Gavaskar.

Perhaps the fellow who menaced Lord Harris with a stick back in 1879 sometimes turns in his grave and wishes the whole thing had never happened. Who knows? But without the odd row and riot, regrettable as some of them are, Test history would have lost a good deal of its colour.

145

Touring

Members of the 1968
MCC team touring the
West Indies relax near
the Barbados Hilton.

Below
**Len Hutton enjoys
Australia's abundant
fruit after years of
post-war rationing in
Britain.**

When Wally Hammond took an MCC team to Australia in 1946, the English players were wide-eyed with eager excitement at the sight of unlimited steaks on their dinner menus.

This was luxury they had not been able to enjoy in five years since the introduction of wartime rationing had taken its toll.

Thirty years later, when I captained MCC on the 1976–77 tour of India, I was joined at a beachhouse party in Bombay by the young Nottinghamshire batsman, Derek Randall. I will long remember and smile over the moment when I caught sight of him across the room, standing with a glass of finest French Champagne in one hand and a slice of toast and caviar in the other.

Derek gave me one of his infectious grins, blatantly basking in this show of affluent indulgence. Then he glanced questioningly down at his caviar and remarked seriously: 'The blackcurrant jam tastes of fish, doesn't it?'

To my mind, these two, seemingly unrelated tales illustrate the vast changes in the character of international cricket touring over the past 30 years.

Cricketers abroad were once surprised by steak, now it's Champagne and caviar – the comparison is not meant to be serious or meaningful but I think it emphasises the arrival of Test players into the jet set.

Naturally, I cannot begin to claim knowledge of the personalities, let alone the eating habits, of the first England team to visit Australia a century ago. But take the steak to caviar situation a few steps farther back and perhaps you will not be far from the truth.

Everything has changed dramatically since those far-off times when men such as Lord Harris and the Hon. Ivo Bligh led the nineteenth-century England teams down under. Means of travel, length of tours, standard of hotels, food and general living conditions are all totally different now – and, in most cases, I have to say I'm glad to be playing Test cricket in the 1970s rather than the 1870s.

There is, I admit, something romantic about a journey from England to Australia by boat – which, of course, was the method

147

of travel used until fairly recent times. It must have been a great adventure and a memorable experience.

Thinking about it all in these terms makes me imagine that maybe, after all, I would love to have been around to undertake that sort of tour. But then I think of my family and I know I am better off in the age of jet airliners, when the trek half-way round the world is cut from seven weeks to something short of two days, a staggering difference.

In the days of sea travel, an MCC tourist picked for a trip to Australia, or vice-versa, would complete the last county match of his domestic season and almost immediately find himself packing his bags, waving goodbye to his wife and family and walking down the gangplank. In most cases, he would not be back on home shores until a few days before the start of the following home season.

There was, of course, no alternative. If you wanted to play for England, this was the life – and I have to say I have heard few of the old Test players complain about their lot. In general, they seem to have thoroughly enjoyed the 'cruise' and the process of hopping between the cricket centres by means of road or rail – a more leisurely, if less comfortable means than the modern method of using internal airlines.

I think the part I would not have enjoyed was the journey home. Once a tour is over and the series either won, lost or drawn, there is an instant feeling of anti-climax, and certainly in my case, a desire to return home to my family as quickly as possible.

Before air travel took over, this was not possible. Even after the final match, an MCC player faced the prospect of several weeks at sea before stepping back onto English soil.

This, I would have thought, must have increased the chances of homesickness – one of the traditional problems incurred by the

Opposite
**Denis Compton
improves his golf during
the long voyage to
Australia in 1950 aboard
the SS Stratheden.**

Left
**Team members Bailey,
Simpson, Parkhouse,
Compton, McIntyre and
Hutton provide some
entertainment on the
SS Stratheden.**

Below
**Mike Selvey shows how
it's done during a break
in the Indian tour, 1977.
Mike Brearley and Derek
Underwood keep a safe
distance.**

touring teams of any country.

Personally, I suffer little from this while on a tour abroad because I find there is always something to do. Boredom is always a problem, and, together with failure on the field, it certainly breeds the feeling that you are in the wrong place and all you really want to do is get back to your wife or girlfriend.

Homesickness tends to strike me in the most unusual places – like Bradford, Manchester or Nottingham. Yes, I get homesick in my own country. It happens during the spells spent travelling around England with Sussex and is caused purely by the monotony of the English cricket system. It is seven days a week, moving from one hotel to another. You can never slow down – and sometimes depression can filter through.

But I confess I have seen some bad cases of homesickness, both on England tours and among the players of countries visiting England.

One MCC player would not have made it through the 1974–75 trip to Australia but for the knowledge that his wife was going to join him in the later stages. He became so depressed and dejected that his cricket suffered, and ultimately it led to his omission from the team.

For this reason, I am in favour of wives being allowed to join their husbands on a tour whenever they can. The argument that they prove to be a distraction to the players is, I believe, heavily outweighed by the morale boost they can give to their husbands.

To operate a successful cricket tour, there are scores of other minor trouble-spots to be avoided, as I found out during my first experiences abroad with England in India in 1972, and had underlined to me when I went back to that country as captain, four years later.

There are those cricketers who intensely dislike flying, although

Brisbane Cricket Ground, in 1950.

I have personally never encountered any bad cases – in this age, let's face it, they would struggle!

Some have a grave fear of water, which can cause some nasty moments because many players spend a good deal of their spare time abroad swimming from the beaches or in hotel pools. I remember an occasion in the West Indies in 1973–74 when I was in a big group of players enjoying a swim off one of the marvellous Barbados beaches. When we looked back to the shore, we noticed Keith Fletcher paddling warily along the water's edge.

Somebody eventually decided it was time 'Fletch' had a proper dip – only to find that he really couldn't swim!

All players have food and climate problems, particularly in India and Pakistan. But we often overlook that the converse applies. When Indians and Pakistanis tour England, they not only

find it cold – they also cannot eat some of our food, and in many cases do not drink alcohol. In some parts of India, one needs a permit to drink alcohol, and on some previous tours I understand from an English journalist that anyone who wanted to drink also had to sign a form stating that he was a confirmed alcoholic!

While food can still be a problem, actual living conditions very rarely are. In most countries, national cricket teams stay at top-class hotels where their every need is catered for. There are still exceptions, but they are decreasing annually.

A typical day in the life of a cricket tourist is now perfectly civilised. Some will rise very early for a dawn fitness workout – Alan Knott, the England wicketkeeper, is one of the most famous players for physical jerks at an unearthly hour – but most will get up in time for breakfast at around 8 o'clock.

A team meeting may be next on the agenda, before a coach ride to the ground. After the day's play, the team will either go directly back to their hotel, or change and shower at the ground and have a beer or two with the opposition. Dinner at the hotel – and most places offer European food for Englishmen these days – may be followed by a reception, or simply by a free evening.

I have toured every major cricketing country with England, except, ironically, the country of my birth, South Africa. Without hesitation, I can say that Australia is the big one for an England player.

England and Australia are the arch enemies of the international cricket circuit and I expect they always will be. They were, of course, the first opponents in Test history, and the ferocity of the rivalry has probably increased, if anything, over the years.

Various controversies involving the two countries have coloured their cricket relationship, as I explain elsewhere in this book. But certainly since the infamous 'bodyline' series of 1932–33, nothing has ever been quite the same. When England meet Australia, there is far more than a cricket match at stake; there is an issue of deep pride, of national prestige. It affects not only the players and officials but the general public of both countries. This, to me, is one of the most vivid features of a tour in Australia.

The full impact of the importance that Australians place on a series against England struck me in the winter of 1975–76. I was spending the close-season in Sydney, combining a contract to play for the grade team Waverley with a series of commercial engagements.

Australia were, at the time, completing a clinical execution of the West Indies and making a mockery of a series that had been billed as the battle for the world championship. A number of Australian people felt sympathetic towards the West Indians and told me that they would like to see them win another Test. I was flabbergasted.

I pointed out that they had been much less charitable towards England when we were taking a pounding out there the previous year. In that series, I reminded them, there had been no talk of hoping poor old England would pick up a consolation victory. Back came the telling answer–'Oh no, that was quite different– that was ENGLAND!'

In the old days of the marathon sea trip to or from Australia, I imagine the players were fit and bursting to get started on the playing side of the tour as soon as they arrived. Now, however, that is quite impossible. After a 48-hour journey through the air, nobody can claim to be ready for immediate cricket action.

Jet lag is a strange condition to contend with, and there have been occasions when I have not felt quite right for a fortnight after arriving in Australia. For this reason, the build-up to a Test series down under is essentially slow.

As I see it, MCC always do an 'inner circle' tour first, taking in Melbourne, Sydney and Adelaide. Only after that do we move into the 'outer circle' and begin the important business of the Test matches.

Traditionally, the first Test is always played midway up the east coast at Brisbane on a ground that owes much to the work of Clem Jones, once the lord mayor of the city. It was largely through the drive and enthusiasm of this man that the ground was built to such high standards. Unfortunately, Mr Jones knew very little about the preparation of wickets–another of his jobs at Brisbane–and one or two of the Test pitches I have seen there have left much to be desired. In 1976, however, a new groundsman was appointed and I understand they are now producing wickets to match the setting and the majesty of this great stadium.

To play the next Test we need to embark on a journey that feels like flying half-way home. In fact it merely takes one across the width of Australia, 3,600 miles to the city of Perth.

Brisbane to Perth involves a five-hour plane hop and a time change of three hours. It has occurred to me that it ought to be a tour apart–it really does not seem part of the same country as the other four major cities on the cricket circuit.

With all that said, I still find Perth a joy to be in. It is a fine city and it has a splendid cricket ground. The Swan River runs nearby and the whole place is lively and picturesque.

The only problem I have found playing cricket there is that Perth appears to possess the biggest flies in the world. It is disconcerting to be batting in a Test match, maybe watching Lillee thundering up to bowl at you, while a horde of flies perform a formation dance in front of your nose. I have often been amused to watch batsmen blowing fiercely to clear the flies from their face as a bowler approaches.

If you are in the field first at Perth you know you must face a

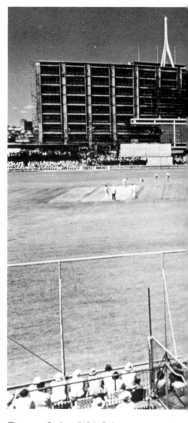

Part of the WACA Ground, Perth.

morning of searing heat without a breath of wind. Almost without exception, the day begins this way, yet by watching the flags on the ground you can usually detect the first sign of change around mid-afternoon.

The flags, which have previously been hanging limply, will stir lazily as the first hint of breeze wafts in from the Indian Ocean. Slowly, the flags' movement will become more exaggerated until finally they are being held out taut and straight by quite a brisk, cool wind.

There are very few other places around the world of cricket in which you can predict a change of weather quite as accurately as in Perth.

Leaving Perth, a Test team will return to the south-eastern population concentration, where the first stop is Adelaide – the city of churches and vineyards. The finest Australian wines are produced around Adelaide and I have accepted a number of invitations to spend rest days in Adelaide in homes on the vineyards. If you like good wine as I do, it's impossible to refuse, however guilty you may feel about it all!

Setting a field at Adelaide cricket ground poses problems, as the cover and mid-wicket boundaries are short, but the straight boundaries seem to stretch forever. When MCC played a pre-Test game there on the 1970–71 tour, Alan Knott was in our

Adelaide Cricket Ground, in 1955 with an Australian rules football game in progress.

team as a batsman and fielder, while his understudy Bob Taylor kept wicket. Knotty was fielding at mid-off and was sent scampering to the boundary after straight drives from two consecutive balls. He reached the first a few feet inside the ropes, ran in 15 yards with the ball – and his throw still did not reach the wicket. The second looked likely to beat him, but Knotty dragged it back with a despairing dive. By the time he had picked himself up and returned the ball, the batsmen had run five – and it could have been seven if Greg Chappell had not been helpless with laughter.

Melbourne Cricket Ground, fourth stop on the Test trip round

Australia, remains one of the wonders of the sporting world – yet to play there can so often be a lonely and emotionless experience.

To me, the MCG – as all Australians call the place – is somewhat featureless. When empty, it conveys little character at all to me. It comes alive only when it is crammed with fans – and whereas some would say that is what it is all about, I must point to Lord's and beg to differ. At Lord's you can sense the tradition and the history of the ground even when you are quite alone there. When I first visited Lord's as a 19 year old it was early April and snow was falling – but I stood and stared in awe. Melbourne could never do that for me, despite the fact that it has been the recognised focal point of Australian cricket for 100 years.

It is a vast, curved bowl, capable of holding 100,000 spectators. When it is full, or nearly full, it is an incredible experience to play there. It can lift you or destroy you. But you can go there with a respectable 20,000 attendance in the ground and play with the notion that the place is empty.

Sydney, venue of the fifth Test, gets my vote as the best ground in Australia. The city also happens to be one of my favourite places in the world. Even disregarding the famous bridge, it is a fairytale expanse of golden beaches and eyecatching waterways.

The cricket ground has more character than any other in the country and it provides the added bonus of great cricket wickets. If every Test match through the ages could be played at Sydney, I would find few complaints.

So those are the Test grounds of Australia – and I make no apologies for delving into far greater detail with this country than I shall any other. If cricket was born and lives in England, it has Australia as a very near neighbour – and has done since the advent of Test cricket.

The only problem for an English newcomer to Australia is to find himself confronted with the locals calling him a 'pommie bastard'. It takes time to accept this, but to my mind it signifies the Australian manner of showing respect. To an outsider, Australians may seem a little coarse, but believe me they do respect the English – it has been said with some justification that the Melbourne society is more English than England itself.

Certainly, the best illustration I can give of a typical Australian cricketer's approach to the game is to repeat the tale of my first Test century, scored at Brisbane on the 1974–75 tour – an innings that I still treasure above any others I have played, purely because it was against the great enemy.

Earlier in the game, I had dismissed Dennis Lillee by giving him a bouncer with my first delivery. Lillee swore vengeance, and when I came out to bat he was pawing the turf somewhere near the pavilion, impatient to get at me. Sure enough, I suffered a barrage of short balls – but I won the day with a ton. Yet through

A bird's-eye view for a lad on the top of the Northern Stand at Melbourne Cricket Ground in 1961.

all the harsh words and rivalry on the field, nothing was carried into the pavilion, and Dennis was soon in the dressing-room pouring out a beer for me. That is not only typical of Lillee, it epitomises the Australian mentality.

If Australia is the number one tour for any Test player, the West Indies must be next in line. Every cricketing country possesses passions and character peculiar to itself. But the character of the Caribbean islands thrusts itself at you as soon as you land, hits you forcefully throughout your stay – and lingers in the memory long after departure.

To tour the Caribbean is to undertake a series of mini-tours around the islands of the West Indies. Some have retained their

charm and beauty, while others, as I write, are enmeshed in a political situation that has added an extra hazard to the cricket tourist.

But everywhere, you still feel the excitement and enthusiasm of the locals, whose adoration of cricket extends far beyond just packing their grounds for every Test match. Wherever you walk on the West Indian islands, you will see boys of every age staging impromptu cricket matches; on the beach, in the street or just up against a tree.

When I toured the Caribbean as MCC vice-captain in 1973–74, I was delighted and astonished by the receptions we received on each island. Wherever we landed, there would be a West Indian steel band hammering out a greeting. Then we would be ushered off and toasted with the local rum punch. Drink too much of that and it's a hangover booked for the Test match!

Between the Tests, of course, there are days off when touring parties can explore the local delights. I indulged in two of my great passions – activities which I am sure visiting cricket teams have been enjoying ever since men such as Lord Hawke and Pelham Warner led the first English sides out there in the 1890s: golf and underwater swimming.

The golf courses of the Caribbean are quite magnificent. The fairways are generally lined by coconut trees which gives a player the advantage of being able to judge the line to the green – and to enjoy a coconut while following a drive.

Often, I would put on a snorkel and plunge underwater to explore the fascinating life contained in the Caribbean Sea. The vegetation and rock formation underwater gives the impression of a series of barrier reefs – and the variety of fish is quite remarkable. One of the other delights of a West Indian tour is that their diet includes a surfeit of succulent fish, fresh from the sea and quite delicious.

The colour of the country extends to the cricket grounds, where the single disadvantage is size. Most of them are smaller than the average Test ground and inevitably they run into problems with crowds.

Barbados, probably the most famous of the islands, houses a ground steeped in tradition at Bridgetown. Barbados has always been the centre of West Indian cricket and this ground has been the home of many of their finest players, including Gary Sobers.

The Port of Spain ground at Trinidad sometimes stages two Test matches in a series as it has a bigger capacity than the others. Spinners tend to thrive here on an Indian type of wicket.

Guyana, where the eye-opening Bourda ground has its buildings carved entirely out of wood, and Jamaica, where the crowd at Kingston are among the most excitable I have ever seen, complete the current Test grounds. But there are others on the

Youngsters watch a match at the Kensington Oval, Barbados.

diminutive outlying islands, such as the Dominica ground which sits in the beautiful gardens east of the Antiguan capital, which are an essential part of the fascination.

The tour which breeds more hysterical comment than any other is India. Before I first went there in 1972, I was warned of the dirt, the disease, the food, the heat – just about everything was intolerable in the eyes of many who had apparently been there. Well, I have now toured India twice and can state categorically that the criticism is rubbish.

Sure, there are problems. And I freely concede that before the advent of the continental-style five-star hotels which can now be found in all major towns, a touring side would have faced more health troubles than they do now.

But I always tell those who frown doubtfully over India that cricketers are basically entertainers – and they will find no finer stage and no more receptive audience than those in Calcutta and Bombay. The Indian public treat a visiting cricket team as English youngsters would treat pop stars – with unquestioning idolisation. They provide hospitality second to none; nothing is too much trouble for the Indians.

On the 1972–73 tour, MCC arrived at Amritsar for our match against North Zone. On our first morning in the hotel, we were served an inedible Indian-type breakfast. We called for the

Pages 160–161
The Wanderers ground, Johannesburg in 1956.

manager and explained that we required an English breakfast, with eggs and bacon. He looked completely blank. That sort of food was simply unheard of in those parts. But instead of brushing us off impatiently, the manager spent the day and night which followed racing around the nearby townships buying up all the English food he could muster. The next morning we sat down to one of the tastiest bacon-and-egg breakfasts I have ever eaten, and when we had had our fill, this co-operative 18-stone manager joined us and ate all that we couldn't manage ourselves!

The early stages of an Indian tour can be unpleasant. A European's body system, or an Australian's for that matter, will take time to adapt to conditions which are totally foreign. I have been in India as long as three weeks before feeling fully fit.

There is so much to see in a land where the feudal class system still dominates. With my Sussex background, I was weened on stories of India told by 'Tiger' Pataudi and his famous predecessors in the county team, Ranji and Duleep. They told of the Maharajahs with their incalculable treasures stored in the palaces which dot the country. But it needs to be seen to appreciate the truth.

Part of the reason why I love going to India is that I have a rapport with the country's cricket crowds. They took to me because I was so very different from their regular diet of short, dark men. Indian crowds long to identify with the players, yet their own stars remain quite detached. I get involved with the spectators – and they certainly appreciate it.

Delhi traditionally stages the first Test. It is a cool, clean city in the northern part of India, and the presence of the British High Commission headquarters provides a haven for MCC teams. The little things that they have missed since leaving England – down to items such as chocolate or marmite – are all catered for, which has always given us a morale boost before the Test.

The Calcutta stadium is one of the finest cricket grounds in the world. It can hold 75,000, and for a Test will comfortably fill and leave thousands locked outside. Although Indian crowds do not drink, as the Australians do, a Calcutta crowd is as noisy as any at Sydney.

Madras is the most southerly point of the tour, and logically the most humid. The cricket ground is quite modern, but fielding in such sticky conditions can be extremely uncomfortable. The England fast bowler Chris Old had to leave the field in a hurry during the 1973 Test there, because he had perspired so much in his opening three overs that his trousers had stuck to his legs and rendered him quite incapable of running.

Then there is Bombay, and the incredible new Wankhede Stadium, a sight that is at once fantastic and sad. It is fantastic because, despite being one of the finest grounds on the circuit, it

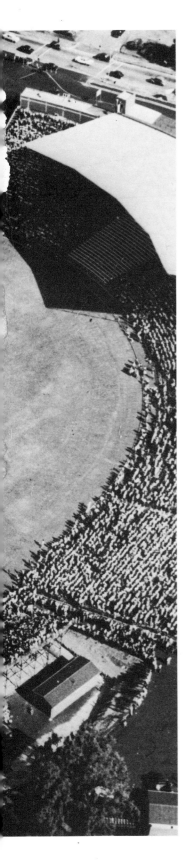

took less than a year to build and cost a 1½ million pound pittance. Sad, because for political reasons it was built next to the ground it has replaced, the Brabourne Stadium. I have scored a Test century at Brabourne, and to me this new move was akin to building a brand new stadium next door to Lord's.

All domestic housebuilding was delayed in Bombay while the Wankhede operation monopolised supplies of steel and concrete – an extreme measure, but one which underlines the Indian fanaticism for the game.

Up to 1977, Pakistan had traditionally formed the second leg of an MCC tour which began in India. So, just as New Zealand suffers from following Australia, it often tended to be regarded as something of an anti-climax.

I have to say that I have not found Pakistan the most pleasant place in the world to play cricket. The heat can sap one's strength completely, and there is also less to enjoy in the countryside, which tends to be more rugged even than India.

Karachi, their foremost Test ground, suffers from regular student riots which have frequently disrupted the cricket. As on Pakistan's other major grounds, Karachi breeds a surfeit of drawn Tests, as the wickets are pure paradise for the batsmen.

Lahore is generally the venue for the second Test, before Hyderabad brings a sting to the tail of the tour. I can honestly say I have never played Test cricket in a hotter place than Hyderabad; but the heat and conditions have at least left me with a number of anecdotes.

When we played there in 1973, both teams scored around the 500 mark in the first innings. We were in the field for three days in the most sweltering heat I can remember. Wicketkeeper Alan Knott was quite severely sunburnt under his chin, of all places, because the sun was reflecting off the parched wicket. I know players who literally thought they were dying as the hours dragged by out there; yet there was one England player quite unconcerned by it all – Dennis Amiss, my room-mate. Dennis fell ill after scoring a century, and each night I would stagger back into our hotel room, absolutely shattered, to find him sitting up cheerfully in bed, eager to know the story of the day.

On another occasion at Hyderabad, Intikhab Alam, the Pakistan captain and idol of the crowds, attempted to quell some unrest. As he walked towards the spectators, however, they rushed over the barriers and mobbed him. When he finally shook himself free, he was covered from head to toe in dust and grime. When the crowd cleared, the area around the mobbing was completely stripped of grass!

The longest trip an English cricketer can make is to New Zealand. But when he gets there, he will feel more at home than on any other part of the cricket globe.

New Zealand resembles England in climate, food and people. As I write this book, it even seems that the New Zealanders are copying the currency problems of the English!

The North Island suffers from a heavy rainfall, often interfering with the cricket. Their Test grounds are Auckland and Wellington. The South Island is comfortably my favourite of the two and it contains one of the most fabulous places I have seen on my travels with the England side. Down on the west coast, away from the centres of population, lies a small town called Queenstown – ironically, the name of my birthplace in South Africa. The view from Queenstown is one that I am sure I will never forget: the emerald green water of an amazing lake, a mountain rising steeply out of the water, and gushing streams flashing down the hillside. If you dare, you can spend a rest day speeding down the mountain streams in jet boats.

Test cricket on the South Island is played at Dunedin, which always reminds me of Scotland, and at Christchurch, the centre of the nation's cricket and the base for the formation of the New Zealand Cricket Council in 1894.

I have mentioned every major cricketing country except South Africa, sadly an outcast from the sporting world at the moment. It used to be said that South Africa was the finest tour of all to go on, both for the country and the hospitality. Although I have never had the opportunity to confirm this opinion with England, my knowledge of the country from birth leaves me in no doubt that it was indeed a very special trip.

The high standard of living there, and the South African people's great love for sport, predictably leads to a situation where the cricket tourist is treated regally. Naturally, I still cherish hopes of visiting South Africa with an England team.

Newlands, the Test ground at Cape Town, revels in a superb Mediterranean climate. With Table Mountain providing the backdrop, it is one of the most picturesque places to play. South Africa's equivalent of the Melbourne Cricket Ground is The Wanderers at Johannesburg, about 6,000 feet above sea level and a splendid stadium. Kingsmead, the Durban ground, is steamy and humid, and houses the famous Castle Corner which can be likened to the Tavern at Lord's or The Hill at Sydney for liquor, noise and humour. Lastly, there is Port Elizabeth, a pleasant spot with a coastal climate.

As a boy, I would wait eagerly for the Test teams to arrive in South Africa. Yet the only series I have seen there was in 1964–65 – another irony, as the visitors were Mike Smith and his England team.

Cricketers, even now, are not highly paid individuals. They need incentives, and touring is one of the features that makes the job attractive.

The Calcutta stadium. The vast crowd which paid to see one hour's cricket on the last day of the second Test during the 1976–77 England tour.

The players with whom I have toured, and enjoyed countless adventures and experiences, have become firm friends. If anything, you tend to be drawn closer to your touring companions than even to team-mates in the county team at home. For four or five months at a stretch you are living together in a group of 16 or 17; every happiness, every misfortune, is shared. It is an emotion that can never be lost, for even when the tour is over and everyone is back home, frequent reunions relive the tremendous times of the past tour. On every trip there will be highs and lows, good times and bad times. Yet it is a feature of the game that will continue to excite and fascinate long into the second century of Test cricket.

Now and the Future

Jeff Thomson bowling during the second Test at Lord's in 1975. A year earlier, he had joined Lillee to form a pace bowling duo which was to transform Australia's fortunes. The batsman is John Edrich.

There is a theory often bandied about that it is impossible for one or two players to transform a team from mediocrity to greatness. But two gentlemen called Lillee and Thomson have proved that if you can bowl at 90 miles per hour, nothing is impossible.

Early in the seventies, Australia were twice destroyed by pace. South Africa's Pollock and Procter ruined them in 1970, England's Snow repeated the treatment 12 months later. The Aussies were ambushed like commandos with no guns – they simply had no-one to return fire.

Then along came Dennis Lillee to wave the magic wand over the team. By 1972, Australia were a totally different proposition. They won two Tests from Illingworth's England, then marched on to demolish the West Indies on their own islands.

Thomson swept onto the scene like a hurricane two winters later and suddenly everyone was hailing the Aussies as invincibles again. Yet most of the batsmen who played the support parts to Lillee and Thomson had been around in those sorry days when they themselves had been undone by pace.

My point is simply that the emphasis of modern Test cricket has swung so far towards the pace bowlers that it is now inconceivable that any country will vie for the top without possessing at least two men in the top bracket of speed bowlers. Without them, they may be far too good for the weaker countries, but when they come up against Lillee and Thomson, or the West Indian trio of Holding, Roberts and Daniel, they have little chance.

The 1975–76 series between Australia and the West Indies promised great things. It was to be a battle of the world's quickest bowlers and the world's most prolific batsmen. But it faded into a one-sided stroll, the Aussies winning 5–1.

That rubber has left me with no option but to go for Australia as currently the number one side in the world, although I still believe that the West Indies have more natural ability. They simply do not channel it onto the field as consistently as the Australians.

Neither side places any reliance on spin for their success – a

Dennis Lillee wearing out his toe caps bowling for Australia against England in the third Test at Headingley in 1975.

telling indication of the current trend of Test cricket. It is a trend that I find disturbing.

Don't think I disapprove of the fast men, for nothing could be farther from the truth. There is a tingling excitement for the spectators in watching Lillee or Holding dash in. And for the players, certainly for myself, there is a thrill in facing up to the challenge of batting against them.

I would be the last man in the world to advocate that the demanding undercurrent of risk and courage that colours international cricket should be removed. But I am concerned for all cricketers' lives, and I want to see any chance of a batsman being

killed in action eliminated from the game forever.

Cricket has always been a game apart. It requires an element of bravery that simply does not exist in sports such as golf or tennis. To me, that means a century against the world's quickest bowlers deserves far more admiration than victory in a five-setter at Wimbledon, or a series of 30-foot putts sunk in the Open. These might be fine sporting achievements–but at no time is there any threat to life or limb.

All that is fine. But when I witness sickening sights such as the New Zealand tailender Ewan Chatfield lying motionless on a Test match pitch–apparently dead after being hit on the head–I know it is time the situation was examined.

It is in the hands of a whole variety of people. The umpires have a significant influence, the administrators must have their say. But in the final reckoning, it is down to the players to put things right.

I believe that a panel of Test captains should be established, to meet regularly and discuss problems such as short-pitched bowling, slow over-rates, players' advertising and other delicate issues–in short, to thrash out the issues that directly involve their players. Findings of the meetings could then be discussed with administrators and feasible solutions formulated.

Again, my meaning must not be misconstrued. I am no activator for player power or anything of that sort. Players have no place dictating the running of the game, but I am convinced they should be allowed a closer involvement in affairs that, after all, affect them first and foremost.

Players and administrators, I believe, would benefit from being in closer contact with each other. We are all in the game together, and we all suffer the consequences when mistakes are made. Closer co-operation must help, for the problems of the game will never fully be solved unless the players want to solve them.

Too many major decisions are taken by committees which include few of the people who have actually got to go out on the field and do the job–the players and the umpires. It is rather like the Geneva Conference trying to sort out the problems of Rhodesia without inviting Ian Smith and the leaders of the other African states for their opinions.

At Test level, it is the captains, their players, and the umpires, who face the fire when things go wrong. So more attention should be paid to their views. If Greg Chappell, Clive Lloyd and the other captains can pool their ideas, the administrators can be guided by them, rather as the management of a factory may be guided when presented with the opinions of the shop-floor workers by the foremen.

My ideal hierachy would contain a number of individuals with a distinct responsibility, without too many committees restricting

A team of BBC commentators covering a match at Headingley, 1971. In shirtsleeves, left to right: Jim Laker, Ted Dexter (partly hidden), Peter West, and Denis Compton.

their flair and drive. But, in England, I believe the national side is best controlled by a selection panel, although I would like to see greater freedom and responsibility given to the chairman.

I do not think it is right that national selectors should be sitting at home in England while the players they have picked are representing MCC on a tour abroad. They should be included in the tour party. Finance may be a problem here, but the solution could lie in my next subject – commercialism.

Cricket is big business and yet, certainly in England, the potential of the commercial side is not exploited enough. It needs someone with a business brain and commercial drive to pull all the strings. In other words, we need a full-time national commercial manager.

Sponsorship and advertising is now an integral part of the game, whether we like it or not. It must be accepted and encouraged within the interests of cricket, because ignoring the benefits would be the height of foolishness.

Rival bidders for Test match sponsorship, television coverage and advertising rights could be played off against each other, their merits and their bids weighed by a man appointed by the cricket authorities. Perhaps that sounds coarse to the traditionalist, rather like committing cricket to a cattle auction. But facts of life must be faced. The game needs money. We need people with advertising talent, the ability to negotiate – people who want to make cricket a rich concern.

For, once the game's finances are healthy, all sorts of channels open up. Money is available, for instance, for selectors to accompany the national team abroad. Money is available for the setting up of a captains' committee. The problems and the worries are slowly eased.

It cannot be an overnight transformation. But cricket must look ahead. We need the best men available, both businessmen and handlers of players.

A BBC camera covering the third England v Pakistan Test at Headingley, 1971. For many years, television has provided cricket with a reliable source of income.

Television falls into the commercial category and there are those who might say it takes people away from the grounds. But I believe television serves a useful purpose, and I only have to think of Calcutta to know why.

When MCC played there in 1977, there were 80,000 happy people inside the ground every day. But outside, standing in the dust listening to the cheers, were thousands more who had been unable to beg, buy or borrow a ticket. They would have given anything to be able to watch the game on television.

The TV companies are doing the game a service in allowing more people to see Test matches. As long as the stage is never reached when their coverage empties the grounds, television will remain a profitable fact of cricket life.

So what are the trends of current Test cricket. What lies ahead over the next few years? One of my most fervent hopes is for an improvement in Test pitches, for I have played on two within 12 months before writing this book that simply were not fit for the game: Manchester, which produced inconsistent bounce that was like a grenade in the hands of the West Indian quick bowlers, and Calcutta, where stroke playing was impossible on a pitch that had been scraped by scrubbing brushes.

In my experience, there is far too much rubbish talked about fertilisers and undersoils on wickets. My solution to the problem can be summed up by quoting the slogan that appears all around India–'More work. Less talk'.

When Peter Eaton came to Hove as Sussex groundsman, he had a problem on his hands. Our wickets really were not good. Peter asked me how he should tackle the situation and I completely took him aback by telling him to treble his working hours.

It was not a request I expected to be taken literally. I was just making the point that wickets need nursing through most hours of the day. They would benefit from the dawn rolling in of the dew that used to happen years ago.

Peter Eaton took up my challenge and worked incredibly hard. The result was that he won the Groundsman of the Year award in 1976 and Hove is now renowned around England for its marvellous wickets.

Groundsmen must be found who are willing to sweat over their job and take a pride in their pitches – then they should be paid a wage to match. As things stand, the wickets are often helping the havoc created by the fast bowlers and encouraging an excess of bouncers that could soon maim or kill.

I have long advocated the wearing of head protection, and my sports equipment company are, as I write, in the final stages of completing a design that will guard the temples. I would like to see such protectors made compulsory, just as crash hats are compulsory in baseball. Not just in Test cricket, either, but all the way down to the grass roots level at school. Putting on a head protector should be as automatic as putting on pads before going out to bat – let's face it, it is far more vital!

Why we protect our feet, legs, thighs, abdomen and hands yet leave vulnerable the one area where a ball can kill is something I have never been able to understand. I feel sure that when it is put right, as I am convinced it will be, parents will be far happier for their sons to go out and start playing the game, in the knowledge that at least their lives are safe.

Deciding which countries will be added to the Test cricket circuit is far less predictable. The two significant factors are whether South Africa will be accepted back into the fold and whether the ICC will grant Test status to any of the new applicants.

South Africa, I am afraid, can never return while they are governed by white people. It simply is not feasible, however passionately the cricketers of other countries want them back.

Sport is a part of politics which never ceases to dismay me. I have a dream that the United Nations will one day pass a ruling giving complete freedom to sport around the world. All countries can play against each other, regardless of the political differences. It may be a wildly hypothetical situation, but if it could ever be achieved, maybe some of the problems of the world would be dispersed by the goodwill sport could spread. Until everyone realises that battles for political power do not belong on sports-fields, we shall get no farther.

It saddens me that a rugby match between New Zealand and South Africa was capable of decimating the field for the supreme Olympic test, the 5,000 metres. The finest track athletes from every corner of the globe should have been out there in the Montreal Stadium that day. But the implications of a game of rugby forced the withdrawal of so many that the race became no more than a substitute for the real thing. Cricket is in danger of suffering a similar split.

New faces on the Test scene, however, should always be welcomed, and I would have no complaints if Sri Lanka were allowed Test status next year. It is easy to say they are not ready to face the full power of the top countries. But one only needs to look back through history to find that exactly the same thing was said about the West Indies, and about India. The sooner they are given the chance to establish themselves, the sooner they will improve.

There are African countries just waiting for a major cricketing nation to tour there. We should not make them wait. Let's send teams out there to give them experience.

All cricket, and all potential players, must be encouraged. It is a sport to beat all sports. A game that demands an iron nerve, and a dash of bravery, in addition to a multitude of talents. Test cricket may seem to have led a pretty long and exhausting life. But it has only just begun.

STATISTICS

A Century of Tests in Figures

(All series completed by the end of 1976 are included)

England v Australia

	Tests	England	Australia	Draws
In England	105	28	28	49
In Australia	119	43	59	17
Total	224	71	87	66

England v South Africa

	Tests	England	S. Africa	Draws
In England	44	21	5	18
In South Africa	58	25	13	20
Total	102	46	18	38

England v West Indies

	Tests	England	W. Indies	Draws
In England	39	14	14	11
In West Indies	32	7	8	17
Total	71	21	22	28

England v New Zealand

	Tests	England	N. Zealand	Draws
In England	24	13	0	11
In New Zealand	23	10	0	13
Total	47	23	0	24

England v India

	Tests	England	India	Draws
In England	25	18	1	6
In India	23	4	5	14
Total	48	22	6	20

England v Pakistan

	Tests	England	Pakistan	Draws
In England	18	8	1	9
In Pakistan	9	1	0	8
Total	27	9	1	17

Australia v South Africa

	Tests	Australia	S. Africa	Draws
In Australia	20	12	4	4
In South Africa	30	15	7	8
In England	3	2	0	1
Total	53	29	11	13

Australia v West Indies

	Tests	Australia	W. Indies	Draws	Ties
In Australia	26	18	5	2	1
In West Indies	15	6	2	7	0
Total	41	24	7	9	1

Australia v New Zealand

	Tests	Australia	N. Zealand	Draws
In Australia	3	2	0	1
In New Zealand	4	2	1	1
Total	7	4	1	2

Australia v India

	Tests	Australia	India	Draws
In Australia	9	8	0	1
In India	16	8	3	5
Total	25	16	3	6

Australia v Pakistan

	Tests	Australia	Pakistan	Draws
In Australia	4	3	0	1
In Pakistan	5	2	1	2
Total	9	5	1	3

South Africa v New Zealand

	Tests	S. Africa	N. Zealand	Draws
In South Africa	10	6	2	2
In New Zealand	7	3	0	4
Total	17	9	2	6

West Indies v New Zealand

	Tests	W. Indies	N. Zealand	Draws
In West Indies	5	0	0	5
In New Zealand	9	5	2	2
Total	14	5	2	7

West Indies v India

	Tests	W. Indies	India	Draws
In West Indies	19	8	2	9
In India	18	9	2	7
Total	37	17	4	16

West Indies v Pakistan

	Tests	W. Indies	Pakistan	Draws
In West Indies	5	3	1	1
In Pakistan	5	1	2	2
Total	10	4	3	3

New Zealand v India

	Tests	N. Zealand	India	Draws
In New Zealand	4	1	3	0
In India	15	1	6	8
Total	19	2	9	8

New Zealand v Pakistan

	Tests	N. Zealand	Pakistan	Draws
In New Zealand	6	0	1	5
In Pakistan	9	1	4	4
Total	15	1	5	9

India v Pakistan

	Tests	India	Pakistan	Draws
In India	10	2	1	7
In Pakistan	5	0	0	5
Total	15	2	1	12

One Hundred Years Around the World

	Tests	Results (inc. ties)	Draws
In England	258	153	105
In Australia	181	155	26
In South Africa	98	68	30
In India	82	41	41
In West Indies	76	37	39
In New Zealand	53	28	25
In Pakistan	33	12	21
100 years total	781	494	287

Most Runs in a Test Series

1.	Don Bradman	974	Australia v England	1930
2.	Wally Hammond	905	England v Australia	1928–29
3.	Neil Harvey	834	Australia v South Africa	1952–53
4.	Viv Richards	829	West Indies v England	1976

Most Wickets in a Test Series

1.	Sydney Barnes	49	England v South Africa	1913–14
2.	Jim Laker	46	England v Australia	1956
3.	Clarrie Grimmett	44	Australia v South Africa	1935–36
4.	Alec Bedser	39	England v Australia	1953

Oldest Players in Test Cricket

1.	Wilfred Rhodes	52 years 165 days	England v West Indies	1929–30
2.	W. G. Grace	50 years 320 days	England v Australia	1899
3.	George Gunn	50 years 303 days	England v West Indies	1929–30
4.	Bert Ironmonger	49 years 327 days	Australia v England	1932–33

Youngest Players in Test Cricket

1.	Mushtaq Mohammad	15 years 124 days	Pakistan v West Indies	1958–59
2.	Aftab Baloch	16 years 191 days	Pakistan v New Zealand	1969–70
3.	Nasim-ul-Ghani	16 years 248 days	Pakistan v West Indies	1957–58
4.	Khalid Hassan	16 years 352 days	Pakistan v England	1954

INDEX

Illustrations appear in bold type

Photographic Acknowledgments

Colour plates
Patrick Eagar, London: 26–27, 28, 61, 62 left, 62–63, 64, 81, 82, 83, 84, 133, 134–135, 136; Mansell Collection, London: 25 left (Reproduced by kind permission of John Player and Sons), 25 right.

Black and white illustrations
Australian News and Information Bureau, London: 20, 23, 33, 39, 47; British Broadcasting Corporation,

London: 168, 169; Central Press Photos, London: Introduction, half-title, title page, 9, 15, 17 bottom, 18, 19, 20–21, 22, 24, 25, 26, 27, 28, 29, 31, 32, 35, 37, 38, 40, 42, 58, 59, 60, 65, 69, 74–75, 76, 78–79, 86, 87, 88, 89, 90, 91, 92, 94, 96, 97, 98, 100–101, 101 right, 102, 103, 104–105, 105 right, 106, 107, 108, 109, 111, 112, 114, 116, 118, 119, 122–123, 124, 126, 127, 128, 130, 140, 143, 146, 147, 148, 150, 154, 156,

160; Patrick Eagar, London: 8, 17 top, 30, 34, 45, 49, 51, 53, 56, 58, 59, 60, 65, 67, 68–69, 70–71, 72, 73, 74 left, 120, 128, 149, 153, 163, 164, 166; Mansell Collection, London: 11, 13, 14, 85, 121; National Army Museum, London: 80; Popperfoto, London: 131, 132, 137, 138, 139; Press Association, London: 12; Sport and General, London: 145; Syndication International, London: 170.